The Story of the World

TEST BOOK AND ANSWER KEY

Volume 3: Early Modern Times

Peace Hill Press
Charles City, Virginia
www.peacehillpress.com

How to Use These Tests and Answer Key

These tests and their accompanying answer key are designed to go along with Volume 3 of Susan Wise Bauer's *The Story of the World: History for the Classical Child*. These tests are designed for those teachers and parents who want to evaluate their students' understanding of the major ideas and dates found within the *Story of the World* text. After your student reads each chapter of the book, he should be given time to review the reading before taking that chapter's test. If you are using the *Story of the World Volume 3 Activity Book*, you should go through the chapter's Review Questions, Narration Exercises, Map Activities, and other complementary projects and readings. These will reinforce and expand your student's knowledge of the material. For more information on the *Volume 3 Activity Book*, please visit www.peacehillpress.com. We recommend reading one chapter of the text each week and taking the appropriate test at the end of the week.

Although *The Story of the World* is intended for students between grades 1 and 6, we recommend that these tests be used with students in grade 3 and up. They can be used with younger students, but you might find that the Review Questions in the Activity Book are sufficient for evaluating your student's comprehension. For more ideas, support, and suggestions, visit the *Well-Trained Mind* message boards, at http://www.welltrainedmind.com/forums.

Photocopying and Distribution Policy

Name _____   Date _____

The Story of the World, Volume 3: Early Modern Times

Chapter 1 Test: A World of Empires

A. Fill in the blanks.

1. In the year 1600, _____ was the king of Spain.

2 _____ was the king of the Holy Roman Empire.

3. _____ was the king who brought peace to France many years earlier.

4. Spanish adventurers who sailed to South America were known as _____.

5. The king of Spain issued special contracts called _____, that gave these adventures permission to sail to South America and take all its gold.

B. Multiple Choice. Write the letter of the best choice.

_____ 6. When Charles was born, he had _____ kings in his family.
   a. two
   b. three
   c. four
   d. five

_____ 7. By the time Charles was nineteen, he had inherited the thrones of _____.
   a. France and Spain
   b. France, the Netherlands, and Germany
   c. Germany, Spain, France, and the Netherlands
   d. the Netherlands, Spain, and Germany

_____ 8. What title did Charles want?
   a. king of France
   b. emperor of Spain
   c. Holy Roman Emperor
   d. king of the Netherlands

_____ 9. Who fought against Charles to keep him from gaining this title?
   a. the king of France, the princes of Italy, and the pope
   b. the king of Spain, the princes of the Netherlands, and the pope
   c. the princes of Spain, the king of France, and the pope
   d. the king of the Netherlands, the princes of Italy, and the pope

_____ 10. Charles hired a group of _____ to attack Rome.

    a. Italian princes

    b. Spanish warriors

    c. French Protestants

    d. German Protestants

_____ 11. Christopher Columbus was looking for _____ when he sailed west from Europe.

    a. China

    b. India

    c. South America

    d. Spain

_____ 12. Who did the Spanish get to work in their mines in South America?

    a. native South Americans

    b. the poor people who lived in Spain

    c. slaves from China

    d. all of the above

C. True or False. Write the word "true" or "false" next to each statement.

_____ 13. When Charles died, his son inherited all of his lands.

_____ 14. The Spanish took five hundred billion dollars' worth of gold and silver out of South America.

_____ 15. Spanish law declared that the pope got a share of every load of gold brought from the New World.

_____ 16. Because so many Spanish people moved to South America, parts of it became known as "New Spain."

_____ 17. Trading gold with the Spanish helped the natives of South America to become rich.

D. Answer the following question using complete sentences.

18. Describe some of the ways the Spanish took gold from South America.

_____

_____

_____

_____

Name _____ Date _____

The Story of the World, Volume 3: Early Modern Times

Chapter 2 Test: Protestant Rebellions

A. Fill in the blanks.

1. _____ grew up in a palace in Spain and was brought up to be a faithful Catholic.

2. _____ grew up in Germany and was taught to be a good Protestant.

3. The people of the Netherlands built _____ to keep the sea away from their land.

4. The Netherlands is known as _____ today.

B. Multiple Choice. Write the letter of the best choice.

_____ 5. What did William learn at the French royal court?

    a. how to speak French

    b. how to plan battles

    c. how to be a good Catholic

    d. all of the above

_____ 6. The people of the Netherlands spent much of their time fighting _____.

    a. the French

    b. the tides of the sea

    c. German Protestants

    d. the pope

_____ 7. Why was William unhappy with the way Philip ruled the Netherlands?

    a. He would not help the people with their battles.

    b. He made laws preventing the Catholics from practicing their faith.

    c. He did not ask the leaders if the laws he passed would be good for the people.

    d. all of the above

_____ 8. What horrifying secret did William hear while visiting the French?

    a. Philip was planning to kill him.

    b. Philip was planning to massacre Protestants.

    c. Philip was planning to kill the pope.

    d. The pope was planning to kill Philip.

_____ 9. What did the Duke of Alba do when he arrived in the Netherlands?

    a He beheaded two leaders and then killed many Protestants.

    b. He made William the king of the Netherlands.

    c. He drove the Spanish out of the country.

    d. He made peace with the king of Spain.

_____ 10. Why was Mary, Queen of Scots, sent to France when she was a young girl?

    a. Her father wanted her to learn to be a good Protestant.

    b. Her mother was afraid the Protestant Lords would try to make her a Protestant.

    c. Her parents wanted her to learn the French language and customs.

    d. Her country was at war with Spain.

_____ 11. When Mary returned to Scotland, she married _____.

    a. John Knox

    b. James I

    c. William the Silent

    d. Lord Darnley

_____ 12. Who ordered that Mary be killed?

    a. John Knox

    b. Lord Darnley

    c. the Protestant Lords

    d. Elizabeth I

C. True or False. Write the word "true" or "false" next to each statement.

_____ 13. After years of fighting, William assassinated the king of Spain.

_____ 14. A descendant of Philip now rules as queen of the Netherlands.

_____ 15. Mary planned to allow both Catholics and Protestants to worship freely.

_____ 16. Mary, Queen of Scots, and Elizabeth I of England were cousins.

_____ 17. Elizabeth held Mary prisoner for nineteen years.

D. Answer the following questions using complete sentences.

18. How did the country of the Netherlands get its name? Why were the Netherlands also known as the Low Countries?

_____

_____

_____

_____

_____

The Story of the World, Volume 3: Early Modern Times

Chapter 3 Test: James, King of Two Countries

A. Fill in the blanks.

1. King James was known as _____ in the country
   of _____, and he was known as _____ in the
   country of _____.

2. The _____ were a group of Christians who wanted to remove all Catholic
   influences from the Anglican church.

3. The three ships that sailed to Jamestown were the _____,
   the _____, and the _____.

B. Multiple Choice. Write the letter of the best choice.

____ 4. James became king of England because _____ died without having any children.
   a. Elizabeth
   b. Mary
   c. George Buchanan
   d. Henry

____ 5. When James arrived in England, a terrible sickness called _____ was spreading through
   London.
   a. Scarlet Fever
   b. Typhoid Fever
   c. the Black Death
   d. Scurvy

____ 6. What did James do that made Catholics angry?
   a. He killed all of the Catholic priests.
   b. He ordered all Catholics to leave the country.
   c. He made Catholics pay a fine for not going to an Anglican church service.
   d. all of the above

_____ 7. Who was Guy Fawkes?

    a. King James's Scottish tutor

    b. a Catholic who tried to blow up the Parliament building

    c. a leader in the Jamestown colony

    d. King James's son

_____ 8. King James is most famous for _____.

    a. dissolving Parliament

    b. his colony in South America

    c. his "King James Version" of the Bible

    d. finding gold in Scotland

_____ 9. What did the colonists who sailed to Jamestown hope to find?

    a. a new route to India

    b. pearls

    c. gold

    d. furs and timber

_____ 10. Why couldn't the colonists grow crops the first year in Jamestown?

    a. There was a drought.

    b. They did not bring any seeds from England.

    c. They did not know how to plant crops.

    d. The Indians destroyed all of their crops.

_____ 11. _____ was the great Indian chief who lived near Jamestown.

    a. Sequoia

    b. Pocahontas

    c. Squanto

    d. Powhatan

_____ 12. Who married Pocahontas?

    a. John Knox

    b. Lord Darnley

    c. John Smith

    d. John Rolfe

C. True or False. Write the word "true" or "false" next to each statement.

_____ 13. King James believed that a king should listen to his people, because the people gave him the right to rule them.

_____ 14. The colonists arrived in Jamestown in the year 1611.

_____ 15. Half of the first colonists in Jamestown died during the first year.

_____ 16. Relations between the colonists and the Indians were not always friendly.

D. Answer the following questions using complete sentences.

17. Why was John Smith frustrated with the Jamestown colonists? What did he think they should be doing?

_____

_____

_____

_____

_____

The Story of the World, Volume 3: Early Modern Times

Chapter 4 Test: Searching for the Northwest Passage

A. Fill in the blanks.

1. When Samuel Champlain crossed the Atlantic, he landed in the country we now call

   _____.

2. Champlain founded a city that is known today as _____.

3. _____ is a large body of water that was named for Henry Hudson.

B. Multiple Choice. Write the letter of the best choice.

_____ 4. _____ hired Samuel Champlain to find the Northwest Passage.
   a. Henry Hudson
   b. James VI
   c. Queen Elizabeth
   d. Henry IV

_____ 5. Champlain convinced the king to _____.
   a. continue looking for the Northwest Passage
   b. send missionaries to convert the Native Americans
   c. start a colony in the new land
   d. all of the above

_____ 6. What problem did Champlain and his men face at St. Croix?
   a. There was no good drinking water.
   b. The land was too salty for crops.
   c. They had no fresh food.
   d. all of the above

_____ 7. After the colony moved to Port Royal, why did the colonists return to France?
   a. They did not have enough food for the winter.
   b. The king ordered them to come home.
   c. The Native Americans attacked them.
   d. They could not find good drinking water.

_____ 8. How did Henry Hudson first try to sail to India?

    a. up through the North Pole

    b. around the coast of Africa

    c. down the St. Lawrence River

    d. between North and South America

_____ 9. What problem did Hudson repeatedly face on many of his voyages?

    a. ice

    b. strong winds

    c. unfriendly Indians

    d. sickness

_____ 10. What finally happened to Henry Hudson?

    a. His men killed him in the middle of the night.

    b. He died of illness during his final voyage.

    c. He succeeded in finding the Northwest Passage, and the king rewarded him.

    d. His men left him in a lifeboat and returned to England without him.

C. True or False. Write the word "true" or "false" next to each statement.

_____ 11. Champlain encouraged the French settlers to marry the Indians.

_____ 12. Champlain met a group of Indians known as the Powhatan.

_____ 13. Hudson's men had so little food that they once had to eat frogs.

_____ 14. Henry Hudson is today known as the Father of New France.

D. Answer the following question using complete sentences.

15. What was the Northwest Passage, and why did so many explorers want to find it?

_____

_____

_____

_____

_____

Name _____   Date _____

The Story of the World, Volume 3: Early Modern Times

Chapter 5 Test: Warlords of Japan

A. **Matching. Match each name with the correct description. (Some names will be used more than once.)**

    a. Ieyasu

    b. Hideyoshi

    c. Nobunaga

    d. Hideyori

_____ 1. He tried to unify Japan by killing anyone who opposed him.

_____ 2. He killed himself so that his enemy could not capture him.

_____ 3. He was Japan's first shogun.

_____ 4. He forced his enemies to take oaths of loyalty to him or surrender their swords.

_____ 5. The people said his motto was "If the cuckoo doesn't sing, I'll kill him."

_____ 6. The people said his motto was "If the cuckoo doesn't sing, I'll make him."

_____ 7. The people said his motto was "If the cuckoo doesn't sing, I'll wait until he does."

B. **Multiple Choice. Write the letter of the best choice.**

_____ 8. Warlike noblemen who ruled sections of Japan were known as _____.

    a. shoguns

    b daimyo

    c. vassals

    d. samurai

_____ 9. _____ were the Japanese knights who fought for the noblemen.

    a. shoguns

    b. daimyo

    c. vassals

    d. samurai

_____ 10. What country did Hideyoshi plan to add to the Japanese empire?

a. Korea

b. Mongolia

c. China

d. all of the above

_____ 11. What did the Koreans use to fight against the Japanese?

a. swords

b. guns and cannons

c. tortoise boats with iron plates

d. all of the above

_____ 12. How did Ieyasu make sure he would win the battle against the Western Army?

a. He bribed the samurai by promising them money and power.

b. He killed all of the daimyo.

c. He secretly promised the daimyo land and money in exchange for their loyalty.

d. He kidnapped the five-year-old son of Hideyoshi.

_____ 13. Ieyasu made _____ the capital of Japan.

a. Edo

b. Tokugawa

c. Osaka

d. Kanto

_____ 14. Today this city is known as _____.

a. Sekigahara

b. Tokugawa

c. Hiroshima

d. Tokyo

C. True or False. Write the word "true" or "false" next to each statement.

_____ 15. Japan is known as the "Land of the Setting Sun."

_____ 16. Hideyoshi came from a rich, powerful family.

_____ 17. When Nobunaga died, four samurai announced that they would help his grandson rule.

_____ 18. The Koreans and the Chinese fought against each other, making it easier for the Japanese to attack them.

D. Answer the following question using complete sentences.

19. What did Ieyasu force the samurai and the daimyo to do in order to build his own family's power? (Tell about three things in your answer.)

_____

_____

_____

_____

_____

The Story of the World, Volume 3: Early Modern Times

Chapter 6 Test: New Colonies in the New World

A. Fill in the blanks.

1. The Separatists traveled to America on a ship named the _____.

2. _____ was an Indian who taught the Pilgrims how to grow crops.

3. The Pilgrims named their new colony _____.

4. _____ was the strong governor who was sent to New Amsterdam.

5. New Amsterdam was renamed _____ by the English.

B. Multiple Choice. Write the letter of the best choice.

_____ 6. When the Separatists left England, where did they go first?
   a. Denmark
   b. France
   c. Canada
   d. Holland

_____ 7. Why were the Separatists unhappy in this new land?
   a. They had to pay high taxes.
   b. Their children began to forget English and their Separatist beliefs.
   c. They were arrested for meeting in churches.
   d. all of the above

_____ 8. What new name did William Bradford give to the Separatists and the other group of colonists who sailed to America?
   a. Strangers
   b. Saints
   c. Pilgrims
   d. Puritans

_____ 9. What was the name of the second colony formed by Puritans in the New World?

    a. New Amsterdam

    b. Massachusetts Bay Colony

    c. New England

    d. Manhattan

_____ 10. The _____ sent colonists to settle near the Hudson River.

    a. English Trading Company

    b. Dutch East India Company

    c. French India Company

    d. Dutch West India Company

_____ 11. What problems did New Amsterdam have?

    a. The people were attacked by unfriendly Indians.

    b. The town began to fall apart, and the governors could not keep control.

    c. No one would come to trade with the people there.

    d. all of the above

_____ 12. Who captured New Amsterdam?

    a. the Dutch

    b. the English

    c. the French

    d. the Portuguese

C. True or False. Write the word "true" or "false" next to each statement.

_____ 13. The Separatists thought they could change the Church of England.

_____ 14. The first Thanksgiving was held in Massachusetts to thank God for the colonists' survival.

_____ 15. The French brought silk, spices, tea, and coffee to Europe from their trading posts in Asia.

_____ 16. According to stories, the Dutch bought Manhattan Island from the Lenape Indians for about twenty-four dollars.

_____ 17. The strong governor of New Amsterdam was famous for his wooden leg.

D. Answer the following questions using complete sentences.

18. What was the Mayflower Compact, and what did it say?

_____

_____

_____

_____

_____

The Story of the World, Volume 3: Early Modern Times

Chapter 7 Test: The Spread of Slavery

A. Fill in the blanks.

1. _____ brought tobacco seeds from Spain to Virginia.

2. _____ were poor Englishmen and women who agreed to work for a colonist who paid for their journey to the New World.

3. The _____ brought the first slaves to North America.

4. _____ was a Portuguese colony in Africa that was named for an African princess.

B. Multiple Choice. Write the letter of the best choice.

_____ 5. What did the English think about the new Virginia-grown Spanish tobacco?

    a. They thought it was too bitter.

    b. They loved it.

    c. They liked the tobacco they bought from the Spanish better.

    d. They liked the Indian tobacco better.

_____ 6. _____ first arrived in Virginia in 1619 and began working in the tobacco fields.

    a. poor Frenchmen

    b. South American prisoners

    c. poor Englishmen

    d. African slaves

_____ 7. The slave trade that went from Africa to Central America, to Europe, and back to Africa is known as the _____.

    a. Trail of Tears

    b. Triangular Trade

    c. Middle Passage

    d. Circular Trade

_____ 8. The first slaves taken from Africa were _____.

    a. prisoners of war

    b. criminals

    c. poor people

    d. the weak and the sick

_____ 9. _____ was an African princess from a kingdom on the west coast of Africa.

    a. Matamba

    b. Mbandi

    c. Ndomba

    d. Nzinga

_____ 10. The _____ attacked her father's kingdom so that they could keep a steady supply of slaves.

    a. Portuguese

    b. Dutch

    c. French

    d. Spanish

_____ 11. Why did her brother drive her out of the kingdom?

    a. He thought she had betrayed her nation.

    b. He wanted her to marry the prince of a neighboring kingdom.

    c. She refused to sign a peace treaty with him.

    d. He was afraid that she was more powerful than he was.

_____ 12. What did this princess do when her enemy tried to make her sit on the floor?

    a. She demanded a chair.

    b. She used a servant as a human chair.

    c. She stood for the entire meeting.

    d. She refused to meet with him.

C. True or False. Write the word "true" or "false" next to each statement.

_____ 13. Smoking was popular in England because King James encouraged it.

_____ 14. The Dutch were the first nation to become rich selling African slaves.

_____ 15. Tobacco was known as "green gold" in Virginia.

_____ 16. The people of Africa never fought against the Europeans who tried to invade them.

_____ 17. Some people think that the great African princess poisoned her brother.

D. Answer the following question using complete sentences.

18. Why was tobacco farming such hard work?

_____

_____

_____

_____

_____

The Story of the World, Volume 3: Early Modern Times

Chapter 8 Test: The Middle of the East

A. Fill in the missing nations, empires, or leaders that have occupied the Middle East. Write them down in chronological order.

        Assyria

1. _____ (nation/empire)

2. _____ (nation/empire)

3. _____ (person)

        Seleucids

4. _____ (nation/empire)

        Sassanids

5. _____ (nation/empire)

        Ghaznavid Turks

6. _____ (nation/empire)

        Safavids

B. Multiple Choice. Write the letter of the best choice.

_____ 7. When the Safavids ruled over Persia, their leader was called the _____.

    a. khan

    b. vizier

    c. shah

    d. sultan

_____ 8. Today Persia is known as the country of _____.

    a. Turkey

    b. Iraq

    c. Saudi Arabia

    d. Iran

_____ 9. The greatest ruler of the Safavids was _____.

    a. Abbas I

    b. Ismail

    c. Muhammad

    d. Seleucus

_____ 10. Which two empires were ruled by the Turks?

    a. the Ottoman and Persian empires

    b. the Islamic and Persian empires

    c. the Ottoman and Seleucid empires

    d. the Assyrian and Persian empires

_____ 11. The Turks captured Constantinople and renamed it _____.

    a. Baghdad

    b. Istanbul

    c. Bandar Abbas

    d. Damascus

_____ 12. What did Murad do to prevent rebels from forming plans against him?

    a. He closed all taverns.

    b. He killed anyone who refused to take an oath of loyalty.

    c. He made the noblemen move their families to the capital city.

    d. all of the above

_____ 13. Murad is given credit for _____.

    a. capturing Constantinople

    b. rescuing the Ottoman Empire

    c. making Persia a great trading nation

    d. all of the above

C. True or False. Write the word "true" or "false" next to each statement.

_____ 14. The Ottoman empire was founded by the Seljuk Turks.

_____ 15. The Seljuk Turks were known for making good roads and fair laws.

_____ 16. Murad was twenty-three years old when he inherited the throne.

_____ 17. Murad was loved and respected by his people.

D. Answer the following question using complete sentences.

18. What problems did Murad face when he inherited the throne of the Ottomans?

_____

_____

_____

_____

_____

Name _____ Date _____

Chapter 9 Test: The Western War

A. **Matching. Match each name with the correct description. (Some names will be used more than once.)**

  a. Charles V

  b. Ferdinand II

  c. Gustavus II

  d. Christian IV

_____ 1. He wanted to be the Holy Roman Emperor.

_____ 2. He was the Protestant king of Denmark.

_____ 3. He ordered the assassination of Albert of Wallenstien.

_____ 4. He was the Swedish king who forced Ferdinand's army to leave Denmark.

_____ 5. His army was crushed by Albert of Wallenstein.

_____ 6. He was the Holy Roman Emperor who divided his empire between his brother and his son.

_____ 7. He was killed in battle.

B. **Multiple Choice. Write the letter of the best choice.**

_____ 8. Why were the German princes so angry at Ferdinand II?

  a. He passed laws to try to get rid of Protestant worship.

  b. He made them pay huge taxes.

  c. He forced them to send soldiers to fight in his army.

  d. He refused to learn the German language.

_____ 9. The German princes in Bohemia gathered in the city of _____ to protest.

  a. Munich

  b. Vienna

  c. Amsterdam

  d. Prague

_____ 10. What did the German princes do to Ferdinand's two officials?

    a. They hanged the officials.

    b. They forced the officials to sign a peace treaty.

    c. They cut off the officials' heads.

    d. They threw the officials out of a window.

_____ 11. Whom did Ferdinand convince to help him defeat the rebels?

    a. England and France

    b. Spain and Austria

    c. Spain and France

    d. Denmark and Austria

_____ 12. Who sent armies to help the German princes fight against Ferdinand?

    a. England and Denmark

    b. Spain and Austria

    c. Spain and France

    d. Denmark and Austria

_____ 13. The _____ finally ended the war.

    a. Peace of Westphalia

    b. Defenestration of Prague

    c. Cardinal Richelieu

    d. Encomiendas

_____ 14. What happened to the people of Germany because of the war?

    a. Thousands of people died of starvation.

    b. Soldiers robbed the people.

    c. Many of their homes and villages were destroyed.

    d. all of the above

C. True or False. Write the word "true" or "false" next to each statement.

_____ 15. Seven German princes had to elect the Holy Roman Emperor.

_____ 16. Albert of Wallenstein was a kind and compassionate general.

_____ 17. The Swedes and Germans formed the Protestant Union.

_____ 18. Ferdinand signed a treaty that said every German prince could decide what religion his region would follow.

_____ 19. The Thirty Years' War actually lasted for 41 years.

D. Answer the following question using complete sentences.

20. What did the king of Sweden do to prepare his men for battle?

_____

_____

_____

_____

_____

Name _____ Date _____

The Story of the World, Volume 3: Early Modern Times

Chapter 10 Test: Far East of Europe

A. Fill in the blanks.

1. Most Japanese people belonged to the _____ faith.

2. Catholic missionaries known as _____ came to Japan to spread Christianity.

3. _____ believed that wisdom came from the inside and that truth could be found in the smallest, simplest places.

4. _____ was the capital of China.

B. Multiple Choice. Write the letter of the best choice.

_____ 5. What did Ieyasu's advisor, William Adams, say about the Catholic missionaries?

    a. He said they would bring peace to the Japanese.

    b. He warned Ieyasu that the missionaries would be followed by the Spanish army.

    c. He told Ieyasu to kill the missionaries.

    d. He said that the missionaries were sent by God.

_____ 6. What was Ieyasu's response to William Adams's advice?

    a. He made a law that no Japanese could become a Christian.

    b. He ordered all of the missionaries to leave the country.

    c. He made Christianity unwelcome in Japan.

    d. all of the above

_____ 7. What did Iemitsu do to prevent the spread of Christianity?

    a. He executed all of the Christian missionaries.

    b. He burned all of the Christian churches.

    c. He closed all of the Japanese ports.

    d. He forced the Christians to pay high taxes.

_____ 8. The Ming emperors and the people they ruled were _____ Chinese.

    a. Zen

    b Qing

    c. Han

    d. Khan

_____ 9. Why didn't the Ming army defend the city when Li Tzu-ch'eng invaded?

    a. They were angry at the Ming emperor.

    b. A plague had killed many of them.

    c. Li Tzu-ch'eng bribed them with promises of land and money.

    d. They were too frightened of Li Tzu-ch'eng.

_____ 10. What did the Manchu force the Chinese to do as a sign of the Manchu's control?

    a. pay huge taxes

    b. wear their hair in the Manchu style

    c. speak the Manchu language

    d. dress in the Manchu style

_____ 11. Why did K'ang-hsi reduce taxes?

    a. He thought it would help him control his empire.

    b. He felt that the government was already rich enough.

    c. He knew the people could not afford taxes.

    d. all of the above

C. True or False. Write the word "true" or "false" next to each statement.

_____ 12. Ieyasu's son, Hidetada, allowed Christianity to spread more than his father did.

_____ 13. The Dutch were the only nation that was allowed to trade with Japan during Iemitsu's reign.

_____ 14. Qing means "pure" in Chinese.

_____ 15. Li Tzu-ch'eng was a postman for the Chinese government.

_____ 16. During K'ang-hsi's rule, China became one of the largest and wealthiest nations in the world.

D. Answer the following question using complete sentences.

17. What problems did the Ming Empire face?

_____

_____

_____

_____

_____

Name _____   Date _____

Chapter 11 Test: The Moghul Emperors of India

A. **Matching. Match each name with the correct description. (Some names will be used more than once.)**

      a. Jahangir

      b. Khurram

      c. Aurangzeb

_____ 1. He was nicknamed King of the World.

_____ 2. He was nicknamed Conqueror of the World.

_____ 3. He was nicknamed World Seizer.

_____ 4. He built the Taj Mahal.

_____ 5. He signed a trade treaty with James I so that English traders would come to buy spices and silks.

_____ 6. He rebelled against his father and kept his father in prison until he died.

B. **Multiple Choice. Write the letter of the best choice.**

_____ 7. Jahangir was known for _____.

      a. having his father's best friend murdered

      b. sentencing lawbreakers to be crushed by elephants or beheaded

      c. putting the heads of lawbreakers on towers by the roads as a warning to others

      d. all of the above

_____ 8. Jahangir invited _____ to India.

      a. the king of England

      b. an ambassador

      c. a Jesuit missionary

      d. the emperor of China

_____ 9. Who helped Shah Jahan rule India?

      a. his father, Jahangir

      b. his mother, Taj Mahal

      c. his wife, Mumtaz Mahal

      d. his brothers

_____ 10. Most of the people in India were _____.

    a. Buddhists

    b. Hindus

    c. Muslims

    d. Jesuits

_____ 11. Aurangzeb spent many years trying to conquer the southern part of India known

    as _____.

    a. the Deccan

    b. Delhi

    c. Bengal

    d. Calcutta

_____ 12. Who helped the kingdoms of this area fight against Aurangzeb?

    a. the English

    b. Muslim warriors

    c. Aurangzeb's brothers

    d. the Marathas

_____ 13. The English built the city of _____ on the eastern shore of India.

    a. the Deccan

    b. Delhi

    c. Bengal

    d. Calcutta

C. True or False. Write the word "true" or "false" next to each statement.

_____ 14. The Moghul emperors were descendants of Ghengis Khan.

_____ 15. It took over fifty years to build the Taj Mahal.

_____ 16. The Taj Mahal is known as the eighth wonder of the world.

_____ 17. Aurangzeb ruled India for almost 50 years.

_____ 18. Hindu law is known as Shari'ah.

_____ 19. Bands of soldiers who fight in sneak attacks rather than as an organized army are
known as Maratha warriors.

D. Answer the following question using complete sentences.

20. Why were the Hindus in India unhappy with Aurangzeb's rule?

_____

_____

_____

_____

_____

The Story of the World, Volume 3: Early Modern Times

Chapter 12 Test: Battle, Fire, and Plague in England

A. Fill in the blanks.

1. During the English Civil War, the _____ supported King Charles.

2. The _____ supported Parliament.

3. A _____ is a country ruled by a king or queen.

4. A _____ is a country where the people rule by electing leaders who will represent them.

5. Oliver Cromwell was given the title _____ of England.

B. Multiple Choice. Write the letter of the best choice.

_____ 6. What happened at Charles I's coronation?
   a. His wife refused to attend the ceremony.
   b. One of the royal jewels disappeared.
   c. There was an earthquake.
   d. all of the above

_____ 7. What caused the English Civil War?
   a. Charles dismissed Parliament because they refused to give him money.
   b. Charles marched 500 soldiers into Parliament to arrest his fiercest enemies.
   c. The Puritans rebelled and refused to pay their taxes.
   d. Charles imprisoned Oliver Cromwell.

_____ 8. What finally happened to Charles?
   a. He was killed at the battle of Marston Moor.
   b. He was imprisoned at the Tower of London.
   c. He fled to France.
   d. He was beheaded for treason.

_____ 9. After the Civil War, many English people wanted to reform_____.

    a. the church

    b. Parliament

    c. the courts

    d. the army

_____ 10. The years of Charles II's reign are known as the _____.

    a. Protectorate

    b. Reformation

    c. Restoration

    d. Renaissance

_____ 11. During Charles II's reign, what disease began to spread through London?

    a. Scarlet Fever

    b. Typhoid Fever

    c. the Black Death

    d. Scurvy

_____ 12. How did the great fire in London get started?

    a. Someone threw a match out of a window.

    b. Soldiers were burning a building to rid it of disease.

    c. A coal fell out of a baker's oven.

    d. The king's oven grew too hot and exploded.

C. True or False. Write the word "true" or "false" next to each statement.

_____ 13. Charles I believed that God had placed him on his throne and that the people should obey him without question.

_____ 14. Oliver Cromwell was never a king, but he often acted like a king.

_____ 15. When Cromwell died, Parliament invited his son to rule in his place.

_____ 16. Dogs and cats were responsible for spreading disease throughout London.

_____ 17. Many people escaped the great fire of London by fleeing to stone buildings, such as St. Paul's Cathedral, that did not burn.

_____ 18. After the fire, nearly one-half of London was destroyed.

D. Answer the following question using complete sentences.

19. What did Oliver Cromwell do that made him so unpopular?

_____

_____

_____

_____

_____

Name _____   Date _____

The Story of the World, Volume 3: Early Modern Times

Chapter 13 Test: The Sun King

A. Fill in the blanks.

1. _____ was Louis XIV's father.

2. Louis XIV was the king of _____.

3. Louis XIV built an enormous palace named _____.

4. Louis XIV chose the _____ as his emblem.

B. Multiple Choice. Write the letter of the best choice.

_____ 5. How old was Louis XIV when he became king?

    a. four

    b. five

    c. twelve

    d. fourteen

_____ 6. What did his people think about their king?

    a. They believed that their king was a god.

    b. They thought that their king should allow their representatives to make laws.

    c. They believed that the king was God's representative on earth.

    d. They wanted their king to listen to them.

_____ 7. Who was Cardinal Mazarin?

    a. Louis XIV's mother

    b. Louis XIV's advisor

    c. Louis XIV's brother

    d. Louis XIV's father

_____ 8. When Cardinal Mazarin died, Louis XIV announced that _____.

    a. Cardinal Richelieu would take his place

    b. he would rule without any ministers to advise him

    c. Mazarin's son would be the next king

    d. the country would officially mourn his death for one year

_____ 9. Why did Louis XIV bring his noblemen to his huge palace?

    a. He wanted to keep them busy.

    b. He wanted to show off his new palace.

    c. He wanted them to help advise him.

    d. all of the above

_____ 10. What tragedy happened to Louis XIV?

    a. His son died of smallpox.

    b. Two of his grandsons died.

    c. He got gangrene in his leg.

    d. all of the above

_____ 11. What problem did Louis XIV leave when he died?

    a. There was no heir to the throne.

    b. His noblemen were rebelling.

    c. Many people had died because of his wars and extravagant lifestyle.

    d. all of the above

C. True or False. Write the word "true" or "false" next to each statement.

_____ 12. A peasant once saved Louis XIV from drowning.

_____ 13. Louis XIV wrote that he preferred wealth above all else, even life itself.

_____ 14. Louis XIV encouraged his noblemen to spend money in order to make them more loyal.

_____ 15. During Louis XIV's reign, his country became the largest and most important nation in Europe.

_____ 16. Louis XIV reigned for over fifty years.

D. Answer the following question using complete sentences.

17. Describe the famous palace that was built by Louis XIV.

_____

_____

_____

_____

_____

The Story of the World, Volume 3: Early Modern Times

Chapter 14 Test: The Rise of Prussia

A. Fill in the blanks.

1. Prince Frederick ruled over the German states of _____ and Prussia.

2. The first German kingdom was known as the first _____.

3. Frederick's son, _____, succeeded him.

4. Frederick's grandson became known as _____.

B. Multiple Choice. Write the letter of the best choice.

_____ 5. After the Thirty Years' War, Germany was divided into _____ little states.

    a. thirty

    b. two hundred

    c. twelve

    d. three hundred

_____ 6. Each one of these little states was ruled by _____.

    a. Prince Frederick

    b. a separate prince

    c. the Holy Roman Emperor

    d. the king of Germany

_____ 7. The Germans thought of themselves as citizens of _____.

    a. Germany

    b. the Holy Roman Empire

    c. their own little states

    d. all of the above

_____ 8. What title did Frederick give himself?

    a. Holy Roman Emperor

    b. King Frederick I

    c. the Sun King

    d. King of the World

_____ 9. Frederick wanted his people to be loyal to _____.

    a. a piece of land

    b. a monarch

    c. a state

    d. the pope

_____ 10. Frederick's son is known for _____.

    a. fighting to add more land

    b. building a huge palace

    c. strengthening the army

    d. founding a university

_____ 11. Frederick's grandson strengthened the Prussian kingdom by _____.

    a. fighting to add more land

    b. improving the German language

    c. strengthening the army

    d. founding a university

_____ 12. The kingdom of Prussia became the modern country of _____.

    a. Austria

    b. Germany

    c. Russia

    d. Denmark

C. True or False. Write the word "true" or "false" next to each statement.

_____ 13. Prussia lay inside the borders of the Holy Roman Empire.

_____ 14. The Holy Roman Emperor crowned the Prussian king.

_____ 15. Frederick had one of the most splendid courts in Europe.

D. Answer the following question using complete sentences.

16. What did Frederick do to make his people think of themselves as citizens of one country?

_____

_____

_____

_____

_____

The Story of the World, Volume 3: Early Modern Times

Chapter 15 Test: A New World in Conflict

A. Fill in the blanks.

1. The colonists of Massachusetts fought against a Native American tribe in a war known as

   _____.

2. _____ was a fourteen-year-old girl who became a French Canadian heroine by defending a fort while her father was away.

3. William Penn joined a religious group known as the _____.

4. Penn founded the state of _____ and named the capital city _____, which means the City of Brotherly Love.

B. Multiple Choice. Write the letter of the best choice.

_____ 5. As the colony of Massachusetts grew larger, the colonists moved into the lands of the
   _____ tribe.
   a. Iroquois
   b. Wampanoag
   c. Mohawk
   d. Naragansett

_____ 6. _____ warned the colonists that the Native Americans were preparing to attack.
   a. Josiah Winslow
   b. Mary Rowlandson
   c. John Sassamon
   d. Squanto

_____ 7. What happened during the Great Swamp Fight?
   a. Most of the Native American warriors were killed.
   b. Thirteen hundred Englishmen were killed.
   c. The Native American king was beheaded.
   d. all of the above

_____ 8. What happened as a result of the war with the Native Americans?

    a. Twelve English towns were destroyed.

    b. Entire tribes of Native Americans were killed.

    c. The English gained more land to settle.

    d. all of the above

_____ 9. Samuel Champlain befriended the _____ tribe.

    a. Iroquois

    b. Wampanoag

    c. Huron

    d. Naragansett

_____ 10. What disease did the French pass along to this tribe?

    a. the Black Death

    b. Typhoid Fever

    c. Malaria

    d. Smallpox

_____ 11. Which Native American tribe attacked the French settlers in New France?

    a. Iroquois

    b. Wampanoag

    c. Huron

    d. Naragansetts

_____ 12. When William and Mary came to rule England, the people called it the _____.

    a. Restoration

    b. Glorious Revolution

    c. Protectorate

    d. Reformation

C. True or False. Write the word "true" or "false" next to each statement.

_____ 13. The governor of Massachusetts did not believe the warning that the Native Americans were planning to attack.

_____ 14. When the Native Americans captured colonists during the war, they would release them in exchange for money and weapons.

_____ 15. William Penn's Frame of Government explained how his new colony would run, and it named four groups of leaders to be elected by the people.

_____ 16. The people of England did not like the new king of England, James II, because he was a Protestant.

_____ 17. William Penn's city became one of the two largest cities in the colonies.

D. Answer the following question using complete sentences.

18. Who were the Quakers, and what did they believe?

_____

_____

_____

_____

_____

Name _____ Date _____

Chapter 16 Test: The West

A. Fill in the blanks.

1. Galileo was one of the first scientists to use the _____,
which is where a person carefully observes the world and then tries to make a theory that explains
his observations.

2. Isaac Newton observed an apple falling to the ground. He named this force _____.

3. The _____ was the period when the ideas of Isaac Newton, John Locke,
and others became popular in Europe.

4. New methods of farming produced the _____ Revolution.

B. Multiple Choice. Write the letter of the best choice.

_____ 5. Isaac Newton agreed with the ideas of _____.

   a. Plato

   b. Aristotle

   c. Galileo

   d. Charles I

_____ 6. Newton believed that the universe was _____.

   a. like a machine that always worked the same way

   b. a huge, mysterious, magical riddle

   c. strange and unpredictable

   d. too difficult to study and explore

_____ 7. Why did John Locke leave England?

   a. He did not like the new ideas that were being taught in the universities.

   b. He was afraid he might be arrested or executed for not supporting the new king.

   c. He wanted to study the new ideas being taught in the Far East.

   d. all of the above

_____ 8. In a constitutional monarchy, the king and queen have to obey _____.

    a. the common people

    b. laws passed by Parliament

    c. the noblemen

    d. laws passed by the church

_____ 9. According to Locke, if a king tried to "destroy, enslave, or empoverish" his people, he should be _____.

    a. executed

    b. imprisoned

    c. enslaved

    d. removed from the throne

_____ 10. What did the "Acts of Enclosure" do?

    a. They required farmers to keep their animals in pens.

    b. They divided the common fields up into smaller private fields.

    c. They forced farmers to divide their large farms into smaller ones.

    d. They required farmers to keep their animals in the village common areas.

_____ 11. Lord Charles Townshend invented a crop rotation that included _____.

    a. turnips

    b. apples

    c. corn

    d. sweet potatoes

_____ 12. Jethro Tull invented the _____ which made farming more productive.

    a. plow

    b. seed drill

    c. reaper

    d. combine

C. True or False. Write the word "true" or "false" next to each statement.

_____ 13. Galileo believed that the sun revolved around the earth.

_____ 14. A philosopher thinks about ideas while an economist thinks about money and how it works.

_____ 15. According to John Locke, every person has the right to seek life, health, liberty, and possessions.

_____ 16. The rulers of Japan and China were very interested in the new ideas coming from the West.

D. Answer the following questions using complete sentences.

17. According to John Locke, how many parts should a good government have? What should each part do?

_____

_____

_____

_____

_____

Name _____ Date _____

Chapter 17 Test: Russia Looks West

A. Fill in the blanks.

1. The ruler of Russia was known as the _____.

2. Peter the Great hoped to sail on the _____ Sea, but it was controlled by Sweden.

3. Peter founded the city of _____ on the banks of the Neva River.

4. Peter the Great is known for making Russia part of _____.

B. Multiple Choice. Write the letter of the best choice.

_____ 5. Who ruled Russia while Peter the Great was still a boy?

    a. his mother

    b. his sister

    c. the royal guard

    d. the prime minister

_____ 6. Why did Peter want a fleet of ships?

    a. He wanted to conquer Europe.

    b. He hoped to sail to the Far East.

    c. He wanted to trade Russian furs for Western luxuries.

    d. all of the above

_____ 7. What was the problem with the port city of Archangel?

    a. Its waters were frozen for most of the year.

    b. It was controlled by the king of Sweden.

    c. The Ottoman Turks would not allow ships to sail in or out.

    d. The Europeans refused to trade there.

_____ 8. What city did Peter capture from the Turks?

    a. Istanbul

    b. Azov

    c. Moscow

    d. Narva

_____ 9. When Peter visited Europe, he _____.

    a. worked at the docks

    b. lived at the royal palaces

    c. wore fancy clothes

    d. impressed everyone with his manners

_____ 10. Who joined Peter in fighting the king of Sweden?

    a. England

    b. Holland

    c. Denmark-Norway

    d. the Ottoman Turks

_____ 11. What problem did Peter face when building his great city?

    a. The land was swampy and muddy.

    b. There were no trees for lumber.

    c. There were no stones for foundations.

    d. all of the above

_____ 12. How did Peter the Great die?

    a. He was killed by his guards.

    b. He was killed in a battle.

    c. He died of old age.

    d. He caught an illness after jumping into icy water to rescue some sailors.

C. True or False. Write the word "true" or "false" next to each statement.

_____ 13. When Peter the Great became the ruler of Russia, the Europeans in Russia lived in separate colonies for foreigners.

_____ 14. Peter attended a Quaker meeting in England and met William Penn.

_____ 15. Peter ordered his noblemen to grow beards so that they would look more like Westerners.

_____ 16. Peter's war against Sweden lasted over forty years.

_____ 17. At the time of Peter's death, Moscow was filled with Western merchants and diplomats.

D. Answer the following question using complete sentences.

18. What did Peter the Great do to make Russia a rich country?

_____

_____

_____

_____

_____

Name _____   Date _____

Chapter 18 Test: East and West Collide

A. Fill in the blanks.

1. The king of the Ottoman Turks was known as the _____.

2. The _____ were his private royal guards.

3. The Ottoman Turks tried to capture _____, the capital of Austria.

4. Their army was led by the _____, or prime minister.

5. Ahmet III was nicknamed the _____.

B. Multiple Choice. Write the letter of the best choice.

_____ 6. When the Ottoman Turks tried to capture the capital of Austria, what did they do?

    a. They made tunnels underneath the walls.

    b. They used catapults to leap over the walls.

    c. They simply waited until the people inside ran out of food and water.

    d. They marched around the city seven times each day.

_____ 7. Who first realized the Turks were entering the city?

    a. German soldiers

    b. a baker

    c. a guard

    d. the Holy Roman Emperor

_____ 8. What is a croissant?

    a. a curved sword used by the Turkish soldiers

    b. a flower that the Turkish king loved

    c. the flag flown by the Ottoman Turks

    d. a roll shaped like a crescent

_____ 9. Soldiers from what three countries finally drove the Turks away?

    a. France, Germany, and Poland

    b. France, Germany, and Russia

    c. Sweden, Germany, and Russia

    d. France, Germany, and Denmark

_____ 10. What happened to Kara Mustafa, the leader of the Turkish army?

    a. He was killed by German soldiers.

    b. He became the next king of the Ottoman Turks.

    c. He fled to Russia.

    d. His head was brought to the Turkish king in a velvet bag.

_____ 11. Who was unhappy with the changes that Ahmet III began to make?

    a. his prime minister

    b. the private royal guards

    c. the religious leaders

    d. the common people

_____ 12. The country of _____ is the last remnant of the empire of the Ottoman Turks.

    a. Bulgaria

    b. Serbia

    c. Turkey

    d. Montenegro

C. True or False. Write the word "true" or "false" next to each statement.

_____ 13. The Turks were followers of Buddhism.

_____ 14. While trying to capture the capital of Austria, Kara Mustafa lived in silk tents with gardens planted around them.

_____ 15. Ahmet III was a great admirer of roses.

_____ 16. Ahmet III's court eventually became more western than the court of Peter the Great.

_____ 17. Ahmet was put in jail by the Janissaries.

D. Answer the following question using complete sentences.

18. How did Ahmet III try to make the Ottoman court more like the courts of the West?

_____

_____

_____

_____

_____

The Story of the World, Volume 3: Early Modern Times

Chapter 19 Test: The English in India

A. Fill in the blanks.

1. The capital of India during this time period was _____.

2. The _____ brothers were two Indian noblemen who killed several emperors so that they could rule India.

3. English merchants banded together to form the _____.

4. The English built forts in _____ and Bengal.

5. _____ led the English army that defeated Siraj, the ruler of Bengal.

B. Multiple Choice. Write the letter of the best choice.

_____ 6. Which Moghul emperor made three decisions that led to the empire's destruction?

　　a. Jahangir

　　b. Aurangzeb

　　c. Shah Jahan

　　d. Bahadur Shah

_____ 7. Which of the following was NOT one of his decisions?

　　a. He made Islam the religion of India.

　　b. He spend his whole reign fighting in the Deccan.

　　c. He refused to acknowledge the ruler of the Persians.

　　d. He gave the English permission to build a trading post in Bengal.

_____ 8. What did Mohammad Shah do when he first became the emperor of India?

　　a. He destroyed all of the Hindu temples.

　　b. He united all of the independent provinces of India.

　　c. He got rid of the two brothers who were trying to control India.

　　d. all of the above

_____ 9. Which Persian ruler attacked India?

　　a. Farrukhisiyar

　　b. Nadir Shah

　　c. Bahadur Shah

　　d. Jahangir

_____ 10. Whom did Siraj ask to help him drive the English out of Bengal?

    a. the Persians

    b. the French

    c. the Ottoman Turks

    d. Mohammad Shah

_____ 11. What was the Black Hole of Calcutta?

    a. an area of the city burned by the English

    b. a prison where the English kept Indian prisoners

    c. a weapon used by Siraj against the English

    d. a small dungeon where many English prisoners suffocated

_____ 12. What happened to the last Moghul emperor?

    a. The English took him under their "protection."

    b. He was killed by the English.

    c. He was defeated by his own general.

    d. He fled to Persia.

C. True or False. Write the word "true" or "false" next to each statement.

_____ 13. Mohammad Shah spent most of his time reading and writing poetry.

_____ 14. When the Persians attacked India, they burned the capital city and stole many treasures including the famous Peacock Throne.

_____ 15. English merchants came to India to get silk, cotton, and indigo.

_____ 16. Bengal began to follow English law and had its cases tried in an English court with an English judge presiding.

D. Answer the following question using complete sentences.

17. What was so unusual about the way the English took over India?

_____

_____

_____

_____

_____

The Story of the World, Volume 3: Early Modern Times

Chapter 20 Test: The Imperial East

A. Fill in the blanks.

1. The Forbidden Palace was in the Chinese capital city of _____.

2. Chi'en-lung was the fourth emperor of the _____ dynasty.

3. The _____ River and the _____ River ran through the center of the Chinese Empire.

4. The imperial _____ was the symbol of the emperor's power.

5. The _____ is a huge dry plain in the northern part of China.

B. Multiple Choice. Write the letter of the best choice.

____ 6. K'ang-hsi was Chi'en-lung's _____.

   a. father

   b. grandfather

   c. prime minister

   d. son

____ 7. Which of these was NOT one of the categories of Chi'en-lung's most important books?

   a. classics

   b. literature

   c. history

   d. poetry

____ 8. Chi'en-lung had _____ copies of the Complete Library in the Four Branches of Literature made.

   a. four

   b. five

   c. six

   d. seven

9. What did Chi'en-lung do to books that criticized the Manchus?

  a. He put them in his library.

  b. He burned them.

  c. He copied them.

  d. He sent them to the provinces.

10. The people of Chinese Turkestan were _____.

  a. Buddhists

  b. Muslims

  c. Christians

  d. Hindus

11. Mount Everest, the highest mountain in the world, is located in _____.

  a. Tibet

  b. Burma

  c. Taiwan

  d. Vietnam

12. What is the name of the small island that lies off the coast of China?

  a. Tibet

  b. Burma

  c. Taiwan

  d. Vietnam

C. True or False. Write the word "true" or "false" next to each statement.

_____ 13. Chi'en-lung loved books more than anything—even more than his power.

_____ 14. A Chinese dictionary published in the days of Chi'en-lung listed over forty thousand symbols.

_____ 15. According to legend, the people of Shangri-La never grow old and never die.

_____ 16. The Dalai Lama ruled the people of Taiwan.

_____ 17. The Chinese emperor sent four "High Commissioners" to help the Dalai Lama rule.

_____ 18. During this time in history, one-third of the world's population lived under the Chinese flag.

D. Answer the following question using complete sentences.

19. Give two reasons why it was so difficult to copy the books for Chi'en-lung's series.

_____

_____

_____

_____

_____

The Story of the World, Volume 3: Early Modern Times

Chapter 21 Test: Fighting Over North America

A. **Matching. Match each war with the correct description. (Each letter will be used more than once.)**

    a. King William's War

    b. Queen Anne's War

    c. King George's War

    d. French and Indian War

_____ 1. also called the Seven Years' War

_____ 2. also called the War of the Grand Alliance

_____ 3. also called the War of Jenkins' Ear

_____ 4. also called the War of Spanish Succession

_____ 5. began when a Spanish sea captain supposedly insulted an English sea captain

_____ 6. during this war the English burned the Spanish fort of Pensacola

_____ 7. began when Louis XIV tried to expand his territory

_____ 8. began when the English and French both wanted to control the Ohio Valley in North America

B. **Multiple Choice. Write the letter of the best choice.**

_____ 9. The English government paid _____ warriors to attack Canadian settlements.

    a. Iroquois

    b. Huron

    c. Mohawk

    d. Naragansett

_____ 10. What title did Louis XIV give his grandson?

    a. King of Denmark

    b. Holy Roman Emperor

    c. King of France

    d. King of Spain

_____ 11. What was unusual about King George I of England?

    a. He was a Catholic, and Parliament did not like Catholics.

    b. He wasn't related to any of England's previous kings and queens.

    c. He wasn't English and didn't speak English.

    d. He reigned for only one month.

_____ 12. Which of these countries did NOT have a colony in North America?

    a. England

    b. France

    c. Spain

    d. Denmark

_____ 13. _____ carried a message to the French telling them to leave the Ohio Valley.

    a. Robert Dinwiddie

    b. George Washington

    c. Edward Braddock

    d. William Pitt

_____ 14. The English Prime Minister named _____ was determined that England would win the French and Indian War.

    a. Robert Dinwiddie

    b. George Washington

    c. Edward Braddock

    d. William Pitt

_____ 15. The city of _____ now stands on the spot where the Ohio River Fort was built.

    a. Montreal

    b. Pittsburgh

    c. Quebec

    d. Philadelphia

C. True or False. Write the word "true" or "false" next to each statement.

_____ 16. France, England, and Spain had settled nothing after the first three wars during this time period.

_____ 17. The French and English colonists got along with each other until the French moved into the Ohio River Valley.

_____ 18. During the French and Indian War, the English conquered Montreal, Quebec, and New Orleans.

_____ 19. The Treaty of Paris ended the French and Indian War.

D. Answer the following questions using complete sentences.

20. At the beginning of the French and Indian War, what advantages did the French have over the English? How did the English change the way they fought?

_____

_____

_____

_____

_____

Name _____ Date _____

Chapter 22 Test: Revolution!

A. Fill in the blanks.

1. _____ was the king of England during the War of American Independence.

2. _____ was a Virginian who said in a famous speech, "Give me liberty or give me death!"

3. When British soldiers fired into a crowd and killed five colonists, the colony leaders named it the _____.

4. The Second Continental Congress made _____ the commander of the American army.

5. The first huge battle of the war took place on _____.

6. _____ wrote the first draft of the Declaration of Independence.

B. Multiple Choice. Write the letter of the best choice.

_____ 7. What did the "Act of Union" do?

    a. It made Anne the queen of England.

    b. It declared the North American colonies free from England.

    c. It joined Scotland and Wales together with England.

    d. It was the first of several tax acts passed by Parliament.

_____ 8. Why did Parliament decide to pass laws requiring the colonists to pay taxes?

    a. They needed money for the king's new palace.

    b. They had spent thousands of pounds defending the American colonies during the Seven Years' War.

    c. They thought the colonists were becoming too wealthy.

    d. They needed money for their new Parliament building.

_____ 9. Which of the following were NOT taxed by the Stamp Act?

    a. newspapers

    b. dice

    c. playing cards

    d. candles

_____ 10. The War of American Independence began in the town of _____.

    a. Yorktown

    b. Philadelphia

    c. Lexington

    d. Concord

_____ 11. In his pamphlet Common Sense, Thomas Paine pleaded for Americans to _____.

    a. break completely from England

    b. stop fighting and sign a treaty with England

    c. ask Germany for help to win the war

    d. sign the Declaration of Independence

_____ 12. Which country helped the Americans in their fight against Great Britain?

    a. France

    b. Russia

    c. Germany

    d. Prussia

_____ 13. In 1781, the British Commander, Lord Cornwallis, surrendered at _____.

    a. Yorktown

    b. Philadelphia

    c. Lexington

    d. Concord

C. True or False. Write the word "true" or "false" next to each statement.

_____ 14. The Sugar Act required the Americans to pay extra money for all sugar and molasses.

_____ 15. During the Boston Tea Party, the colonists paid a group of Indians to dump 342 chests of tea into the Boston Harbor.

_____ 16. The British sent soldiers known as Minutemen to fight against the colonists.

_____ 17. Paul Revere warned the Americans that British soldiers were on the way to seize American weapons at Concord.

_____ 18. The Americans suffered a huge defeat at the Delaware River in 1776.

_____ 19. In 1783, the British signed an agreement giving the colonies independence.

D. Answer the following question using complete sentences.

20. What did the colonists mean when they said, "No taxation without representation!"?

_____

_____

_____

_____

_____

The Story of the World, Volume 3: Early Modern Times

Chapter 23 Test: The New Country

A. Fill in the blanks.

1. A _____ is a set of rules explaining how a country will work.

2. A _____ government has the power to act for all of the states.

3. _____ is responsible for making laws for the United States of America. It is made up of two "houses" called the _____ and the _____.

4. George Washington chose four men to help him run the country. These men became known as the President's _____.

B. Multiple Choice. Write the letter of the best choice.

_____ 5. How many American colonies became states?

a. nine

b. thirteen

c. twelve

d. fifteen

_____ 6. The different states disagreed over _____.

a. what type of money to use

b. foreign treaties

c. how to pay back France for the money borrowed during the revolution

d. all of the above

_____ 7. The Constitutional Convention took place in the city of _____.

a. New York

b. Philadelphia

c. Williamsburg

d. Washington, D.C.

_____ 8. The President belongs to the _____ branch of the government.

a. legislative

b. executive

c. judicial

d. federal

____ 9. The Supreme Court belongs to the _____ branch of the government.

     a. legislative

     b. executive

     c. judicial

     d. federal

____ 10. Why did George Washington not want to be the first president?

     a. He thought the Constitution was a "horridly frightful document."

     b. He wanted the colonies to remain a part of Great Britain.

     c. He wanted to stay on his farm in Virginia.

     d. He thought he had already fulfilled his duty to the people of the United States.

____ 11. Washington was inaugurated as the first president in the city of _____.

     a. New York

     b. Philadelphia

     c. Williamsburg

     d. Washington, D.C.

____ 12. Which of the following was NOT one of the positions created by George Washington to assist the president?

     a. Secretary of State

     b. Secretary of the Treasury

     c. Secretary of Education

     d. Attorney General

C. True or False. Write the word "true" or "false" next to each statement.

_____ 13. Seven states had to ratify, or accept, the Constitution before it became law.

_____ 14. The President has the power to veto any law.

_____ 15. George Washington served only one term as President of the United States.

_____ 16. Washington convinced Virginia and Maryland to give up a little bit of land between them for the new capital city.

_____ 17. Washington chose the title "Mr. President" for himself.

_____ 18. Thomas Jefferson was the first Vice-President.

D. Answer the following question using complete sentences.

19. What is the Bill of Rights?

_____

_____

_____

_____

_____

_____

Name _____   Date _____

The Story of the World, Volume 3: Early Modern Times

Chapter 24 Test: Sailing South

A. Fill in the blanks.

1. Captain James Cook was hired by the English government to sail to Tahiti and look at the planet _____.

2. When Captain Cook discovered Australia, he named the place where he landed _____ _____ because of the many strange new plants he saw.

3. He explored the coast of Australia and called the land _____ because it reminded him of one of the parts of Great Britain.

4. When England lost the American colonies, it began to send its prisoners to ancient ships moored in the rivers called _____.

5. The first English colony in Australia was named _____.

6. The _____ were the natives who lived in Australia.

B. Multiple Choice. Write the letter of the best choice.

_____   7. After sailing to Tahiti, Captain Cook's secret mission was to _____.
   a. find the Northwest Passage
   b. sail south and find the Great Southern Continent
   c. sail south to Antarctica
   d. study the plant life of Tahiti

_____   8. Captain Cook and his men sailed around two large mountainous islands that form the country of _____.
   a. Australia
   b. Antarctica
   c. Hawaii
   d. New Zealand

_____   9. The people of Hawaii treated Captain Cook well because _____.
   a. he told them King George had sent him
   b. they thought he was a god
   c. he brought them gold and silver trinkets
   d. all of the above

_____ 10. What finally happened to Captain Cook?

       a. He was killed by some of his own sailors.

       b. He froze to death while exploring Antarctica.

       c. Hawaiian natives killed him.

       d. No one knows what became of him.

_____ 11. The first English people to settle in Australia were _____.

       a. prisoners

       b. Puritans

       c. scientists

       d. sailors

_____ 12. _____ was the first governor of Australia.

       a. James Ruse

       b. Sydney Cove

       c. Francis Greenway

       d. Arthur Phillip

_____ 13. Many squatters made good money by sending _____ to London to sell.

       a. coral

       b. wool

       c. gold

       d. timber

C. True or False. Write the word "true" or "false" next to each statement.

_____ 14. When Captain Cook sailed to Tahiti, it was his first voyage at sea.

_____ 15. Captain Cook's ship ran aground on the Great Barrier Reef.

_____ 16. The first English colony in Australia prospered immediately due to the colonists' hard work.

_____ 17. The women greatly outnumbered the men in Australia.

_____ 18. As the English claimed more land in Australia, the natives lost their land and their population shrank.

D. Answer the following question using complete sentences.

19. What was life like for the squatters in Australia?

_____

_____

_____

_____

_____

The Story of the World, Volume 3: Early Modern Times

Chapter 25 Test: Revolution Gone Sour

A. Fill in the blanks.

1. _____ was the unpopular wife of Louis XVI.

2. When delegates came to Versailles to discuss new taxes, the Third Estate renamed the meeting the _____.

3. Members of this meeting took an oath called the _____, swearing to make a new Constitution.

4. On July 14th , 1789, the people of Paris stormed the _____ to find gunpowder.

5. After this revolt, every Frenchman was given the title _____.

B. Multiple Choice. Write the letter of the best choice.

____ 6. Louis XIV and Louis XV became unpopular with the French people by _____.

   a. forcing them to become Protestants

   b. taking away their farms

   c. making them pay more and more taxes

   d. requiring them to serve in the army

____ 7. Why was the French queen so unpopular?

   a. She was a cruel and hateful woman.

   b. She spent millions of French francs while the poor people of France suffered.

   c. She laughed when she heard that French people were starving.

   d. all of the above

____ 8. When delegates from each estate came to Versailles to discuss new taxes, why did members of the Third Estate feel unimportant?

   a. They were told to wear black clothes.

   b. They were only allowed to use the side doors.

   c. There were no reserved seats for them at a special church service.

   d. all of the above

____ 9. The _____ secretly hoped that the king would return to the throne.

    a. Democrats

    b. Huguenots

    c. Republicans

    d. Royalists

____ 10. _____ threatened to invade France if any harm came to the king.

    a. Prussia

    b. England

    c. Denmark

    d. Spain

____ 11. What did Robespierre do to anyone he thought was disloyal to the new Republic?

    a. He imprisoned them.

    b. He executed them.

    c. He banished them.

    d. He took away their land.

____ 12. What finally happened to Robespierre?

    a. He fled to Prussia.

    b. He was imprisoned for the rest of his life.

    c. He was arrested and beheaded.

    d. He disappeared and was never seen again.

C. True or False. Write the word "true" or "false" next to each statement.

_____ 13. After the American Revolution, the French people believed that their king had a divine right to rule France.

_____ 14. Most of the French people belonged to the Third Estate.

_____ 15. When France decided to become a republic, the new governing body became known as the National Convention.

_____ 16. As Louis XVI was led to the guillotine, he urged his son not to seek revenge for his death.

_____ 17. During the Reign of Terror, only people who were loyal to the king were executed.

D. Answer the following question using complete sentences.

18. Who belonged to each of the three estates of the French people?

_____

_____

_____

_____

_____

The Story of the World, Volume 3: Early Modern Times

Chapter 26 Test: Catherine the Great

A. Fill in the blanks.

1. Catherine the Great was not Russian. Her father was from _____
and her mother was from _____.

2. Shortly after Catherine and Peter were engaged, he came down with _____.

3. Peter had always loved the _____ army and forced the Russian army to
dress, march, and fight like it.

4. The head priest of the Russian Orthodox Church, the _____,
pronounced Catherine the Empress of Russia.

B. Multiple Choice. Write the letter of the best choice.

_____ 5. _____ invited Catherine to come to Russia.
   a. Peter Ulrich
   b. Empress Elizabeth
   c. Peter the Great
   d. the royal guard

_____ 6. Catherine first traveled to the Russian capital city of _____.
   a. Archangel
   b. Narva
   c. Moscow
   d. St. Petersburg

_____ 7. Why did Catherine dislike Peter?
   a. He was rude to the servants and courtiers.
   b. He made unpleasant noises and loud jokes in church.
   c. He refused to speak Russian.
   d. all of the above

_____ 8. After her wedding, Catherine spent many hours reading books about _____.
   a. history and philosophy
   b. military tactics
   c. the emperors of Rome
   d. all of the above

_____ 9. What did Catherine do when Empress Elizabeth died?

    a. She went to the cathedral every day to mourn.

    b. She immediately claimed the throne for herself.

    c. She paid the army to overthrow her husband.

    d. She threw huge feasts and told the court not to wear mourning clothes.

_____ 10. Where did Peter get money for the royal treasury?

    a. He sold many of the imperial jewels.

    b. He sold peasants as slaves to Russia's enemies.

    c. He sold land that belonged to the Russian Orthodox Church.

    d. He borrowed money from one of Russia's enemies.

_____ 11. Who gained the most power during Catherine's reign?

    a. the peasants and serfs

    b. the priests

    c. the Turks

    d. the noblemen

C. True or False. Write the word "true" or "false" next to each statement.

_____ 12. Catherine's parents were both thrilled that she might one day be the queen of Russia.

_____ 13. Empress Elizabeth was a large, frightening woman who flew into rages at her servants.

_____ 14. Catherine was not allowed to see her newborn baby for six weeks.

_____ 15. Peter supposedly died in a fight with one of his guards, but it appeared that he had been strangled.

_____ 16. Catherine wanted her people to have the same rights as citizens of the United States and France.

D. Answer the following question using complete sentences.

17. What Western ideas and practices did Catherine the Great bring to Russia?

_____

_____

_____

_____

_____

Name _____   Date _____

The Story of the World, Volume 3: Early Modern Times

Chapter 27 Test: A Changing World

A. Fill in the blanks.

1. In 1769 _____ perfected the steam engine.

2. A steam engine would run as long as it had _____ for fuel.

3. Cotton was the main crop grown in the _____ part of the United States.

4. Eli Whitney invented the _____ to separate seeds from the cotton.

5. Whitney had another idea that we now call _____, which means that parts are interchangeable.

B. Multiple Choice. Write the letter of the best choice.

_____ 6. Before the steam engine was invented, what did people use for power?

    a. muscles

    b. water

    c. wind

    d. all of the above

_____ 7. A steam engine works by heating water in a closed metal bowl called a _____.

    a. boiler

    b. cylinder

    c. piston

    d. boiling pot

_____ 8. As the water is heated, it turns into steam, which is pushed out of the metal bowl through a narrow pipe called a _____.

    a. boiler

    b. piston

    c. cylinder

    d. screw

_____ 9. What danger did coal miners face?

    a. They could be killed by explosions or tunnel collapse.

    b. They could suffocate in the small damp tunnels.

    c. They might develop "blacklung" from years of breathing coal dust.

    d. all of the above

_____ 10. Why did it take a long time to fix a gun in America?

    a. The parts of each gun fit only that gun and no other.

    b. The parts for American guns had to be ordered from England.

    c. There were very few gunsmiths in America.

    d. all of the above

_____ 11. Who asked Eli Whitney to build a gun factory?

    a. the French government

    b. the American government

    c. the English government

    d. the East India Company

_____ 12. Which of the following was NOT made with interchangeable parts?

    a. clocks

    b. farm machinery

    c. guns

    d. jewelry

C. True or False. Write the word "true" or "false" next to each statement.

_____ 13. Only men were allowed to work in the coal mines.

_____ 14. Farmers did not like the idea of railroads crossing through their lands.

_____ 15. Using Eli Whitney's invention, a single worker could clean fifteen or twenty pounds of cotton per day.

_____ 16. Eli Whitney was the first person to think of interchangeable parts.

_____ 17. The idea of interchangeable parts helped spread factories across North America.

D. Answer the following question using complete sentences.

18. How did the steam engine change life in England, Europe, and North America?

_____

_____

_____

_____

_____

The Story of the World, Volume 3: Early Modern Times

Chapter 28 Test: China and the Rest of the World

A. Fill in the blanks.

1. _____ taught that the Chinese should accept nature and learn from it in a harmonious way, not try to master it.

2. Chi'en-lung only allowed foreign ships to enter the port of _____.

3. _____ was England's ambassador to China.

4. The ambassador was expected to _____, which means he had to get down on his hands and knees and knock his forehead against the floor to show the emperor's greatness.

5. The English made a drug called opium from _____ juice.

B. Multiple Choice. Write the letter of the best choice.

_____ 6. The Chinese called themselves the _____.
   a. Center of the Universe
   b. Open Door Civilization
   c. Land of the Setting Sun
   d. Central Civilization

_____ 7. What did the English merchants want to buy from China?
   a. tea, silk, and spices
   b. tea, cotton, and coffee
   c. silk, spices, and bamboo
   d. silk, cotton, and porcelain

_____ 8. What did Chi'en-lung do with the gifts brought by the English ambassador?
   a. He sent them back to England.
   b. He burned them.
   c. He ordered that they be left at a summer palace.
   d. He distributed them among his officials.

_____ 9. Which of the following was NOT one of King George's requests?

    a. He wanted Chi'en-lung to allow an ambassador to live in Peking.

    b. He wanted British ships to be able to sail into all of China's ports.

    c. He wanted to build trading posts and settlements in China.

    d. He wanted Chi'en-lung to send a Chinese ambassador to live in London.

_____ 10. Where did the English grow the plant used to make opium?

    a. North America

    b. India

    c. Scotland

    d. China

_____ 11. Which of the following is NOT true about opium?

    a. People who took it felt at peace.

    b. It made patients dull and confused.

    c. It gave people nightmares when they took it.

    d. The more patients took it, the less it worked, so they needed more and more.

_____ 12. How did the Chinese begin to use opium?

    a. They smoked it in pipes.

    b. They pressed it into tablets.

    c. They stirred it into syrup.

    d. They sprinkled it on their food.

C. True or False. Write the word "true" or "false" next to each statement.

_____ 13. Chi'en-lung accepted every request made by King George.

_____ 14. English doctors used opium to treat patients who were in pain.

_____ 15. Samuel Taylor Coleridge's poem about Xanadu doesn't make sense because he was under the influence of opium when he wrote it.

_____ 16. Chi'en-lung made opium illegal, but the British continued to smuggle it into China.

_____ 17. Only the rich people of China used opium.

D. Answer the following question using complete sentences.

18. What were the Eight Regulations? (Write about two of the Regulations in your answer.)

_____

_____

_____

_____

_____

Name _____   Date _____

Chapter 29 Test: The Rise of Bonaparte

A. Fill in the blanks.

1. After the French Revolution, French leaders were put into two houses called the Council of _____ and the Council of _____.

2. These two houses named a five-man committee called the _____ to rule France.

3. When Napoleon needed money, he sold the _____ to the United States for fifteen million dollars.

4. _____ was the commander of the British fleet when Napoleon tried to invade Great Britain.

5. Under his command, England defeated the French at the Battle of _____.

B. Multiple Choice. Write the letter of the best choice.

_____ 6. An oligarchy is a country where _____.
   a. all of the citizens are allowed to vote
   b. one person rules the rest of the citizens
   c. only some of the citizens have power to rule
   d. the religious leaders have the power to rule

_____ 7. Who chose Napoleon to lead an attack on Austria?
   a. the five-man committee that ruled France
   b. the two houses of French leaders
   c. the French people
   d. no one, Napoleon acted on his own

_____ 8. How did Napoleon inspire his tired troops to attack Italy?
   a. He promised to double their salaries.
   b. He said they would find honor, glory, and wealth in towns they conquered.
   c. He told them they could have free land in the towns they conquered.
   d. He threatened to kill them if they did not follow him.

_____ 9. What did Napoleon announce to the Italians?

    a. He said he had come to set them free from their Austrian captors.

    b. He claimed their land for the people of France.

    c. He told them that God had sent him.

    d. He demanded that they give him all of their treasures.

_____ 10. What country did Napoleon invade next after his victory over the Austrians?

    a. Prussia

    b. Egypt

    c. Spain

    d. Great Britain

_____ 11. When Napoleon returned to Paris, he replaced the five-man committee that had ruled France with three _____.

    a. consuls

    b. directors

    c. dictators

    d. admirals

_____ 12. What title did Napoleon proclaim for himself at his coronation ceremony?

    a. Dictator

    b. Emperor

    c. King

    d. Holy Roman Emperor

C. True or False. Write the word "true" or "false" next to each statement.

_____ 13. After the French Revolution, all men were allowed to vote in France.

_____ 14. When Napoleon invaded Italy, he respected the Catholic Church and did not take any of its treasures.

_____ 15. Napoleon promised to pay Catholic priests appointed by the Church as long as the priests swore loyalty to him.

_____ 16. Under Napoleon's new laws, women had no rights.

_____ 17. When Napoleon attacked Great Britain, he lost most of the boats he built to ferry his soldiers across the English Channel.

D. Answer the following questions using complete sentences.

18. Who wrote the new constitution for France? What powers did it give to Napoleon?

_____

_____

_____

_____

_____

The Story of the World, Volume 3: Early Modern Times

Chapter 30 Test: Freedom in the Caribbean

A. Fill in the blanks.

1. The people of St. Domingue grew _____ and squeezed the juice from the stalks.

2. They also grew almost half of the world's supply of _____.

3. _____ killed four thousand soldiers in four weeks.

4. St. Domingue was renamed _____.

B. Multiple Choice. Write the letter of the best choice.

_____ 5. Which of the following does NOT describe the French planters?

    a. They lived like French aristocrats.

    b. They gave elaborate balls and parties.

    c. They had to work hard on their plantations.

    d. They lived in huge mansions and spent lots of money.

_____ 6. Who told the slaves stories about the revolutions in France and in America?

    a. the French planters

    b. African priests

    c. Spanish sailors

    d. American missionaries

_____ 7. What did the slaves do on August 20th, 1791?

    a. They burned the planters' mansions.

    b. They killed every planter they could find.

    c. They wrecked the fields where they worked.

    d. all of the above

_____ 8. Who organized the slaves into an army?

    a. Jean-Jacques Dessaline

    b. Toussaint L'Ouverture

    c. Charles Victor Emmanuel Leclerc

    d. Maximilien de Robespierre

_____ 9. What country helped drive the French out of St. Domingue the first time?

   a. Prussia

   b. the United States

   c. Spain

   d. Great Britain

_____ 10. Whom did Napoleon send to St. Domingue to reconquer it?

   a. Jean-Jacques Dessaline

   b. Toussaint L'Ouverture

   c. Charles Victor Emmanuel Leclerc

   d. Maximilien de Robespierre

_____ 11. What country helped drive the French out of St. Domingue the second time?

   a. Prussia

   b. the United States

   c. Spain

   d. Great Britain

C. True or False. Write the word "true" or "false" next to each statement.

_____ 12. There were half a million African slaves in St. Domingue before the revolt.

_____ 13. When the slaves first revolted, they had a good strategy for making St. Domingue free.

_____ 14. Napoleon planned on returning all of the ex-slaves to slavery.

_____ 15. When St. Domingue finally gained its independence, an ex-slave became its first ruler.

D. Answer the following question using complete sentences.

16. How did the rights of slaves in France differ from the rights of slaves in St. Domingue?

_____

_____

_____

_____

_____

Name _____ Date _____

The Story of the World, Volume 3: Early Modern Times

Chapter 31 Test: A Different Kind of Rebellion

A. Fill in the blanks.

1. _____ allowed machines to work without ever having to stop.

2. An _____ made sure that factory workers spent all of their time working hard.

3. English factories that produced cloth were called _____.

4. _____ led the underground army that opposed the rise of factories.

5. Factories were built in the United States near _____ and _____.

B. Multiple Choice. Write the letter of the best choice.

_____ 6. Why was factory-made cloth cheaper than hand-made cloth?
   a. Factory-made cloth used cheaper materials.
   b. Machines in factories could make cloth faster than people could by hand.
   c. Handmade cloth required more expensive tools.
   d. all of the above

_____ 7. When weavers who worked at home could no longer get people to buy their cloth, what did they do?
   a. They became farmers instead.
   b. They started sending their cloth to other countries to sell.
   c. They were forced to go work in the factories.
   d. They joined with other weavers to open their own factories.

_____ 8. How was a factory worker paid?
   a. He was paid for each piece he made.
   b. He was given free cloth rather than money.
   c. He was paid a yearly salary.
   d. He was paid by the hour.

_____ 9. How were the working conditions of the factory difficult for the children who worked there?

    a. They had to work long hours.

    b. They had to stand all day in front of machines.

    c. They breathed in the fine white dust from the cotton, which hurt their lungs.

    d. All of the above

_____ 10. When the British government made laws to improve factory working conditions, who protested?

    a. rich factory owners

    b. weavers and spinners

    c. sea merchants

    d. families in the country

_____ 11. Who were the Luddites?

    a. rich men who made money from the factories

    b. weavers and spinners who started their own factories

    c. people who were angry because their whole way of life was changing

    d. children who were forced to work in factories

C. True or False. Write the word "true" or "false" next to each statement.

_____ 12. Before factories became common, most people worked at home along with their whole families.

_____ 13. Workers in factories sometimes had to pay fines for looking out of windows, speaking to each other, or taking more than fifteen minutes to eat a meal.

_____ 14. Thomas Jefferson thought that factories would be good for the country.

_____ 15. Factory owners built nice houses near the factories for their workers.

D. Answer the following question using complete sentences.

16. How was work in factories different from work in the home?

_____

_____

_____

_____

_____

The Story of the World, Volume 3: Early Modern Times

Chapter 32 Test: The Opened West

A. Fill in the blanks.

1. President _____ bought the Louisiana Territory from Napoleon.

2. _____ was an Indian woman who helped Lewis and Clark.

3. The _____ is a ridge that runs down the middle of North America.

4. _____ was a Shawnee Indian who led raids against white towns and forts in the Northwest Territory.

5. _____ was the governor of the Indiana Territory who convinced tribal chiefs to sign a land treaty and sell their land for a very low price.

B. Multiple Choice. Write the letter of the best choice.

____ 6. Which of the following was NOT one of the territories east of the Mississippi?

    a. the Indiana Territory

    b. the Northwest Territory

    c. the Oklahoma Territory

    d. the Mississippi Territory

____ 7. Lewis and Clark were hired by the President to _____.

    a. find the Northwest Passage

    b. befriend the Indians who lived in the Louisiana Territory

    c. conquer the land west of the Louisiana Territory for the United States

    d. map the land west of the Mississippi River

____ 8. Lewis and Clark built their first winter camp with the _____ tribe.

    a. Shoshone

    b. Mandan

    c. Sioux

    d. Choctaw

_____ 9. What did Lewis hope to buy from the Shoshone Indians to help with the journey?

a. horses

b. food

c. guns

d. hunting dogs

_____ 10. What large body of water did Lewis and Clark find?

a. the Mississippi River

b. the Great Lakes

c. the Gulf of Mexico

d. the Pacific Ocean

_____ 11. What did Lewis and Clark do that would help people who wanted to head west in the future?

a. They made treaties with all of the Indian tribes.

b. They built many forts all along their journey.

c. They made detailed maps.

d. all of the above

_____ 12. What did the Prophet tell his warriors so that they would attack the soldiers encamped at the Tippecanoe River?

a. His magic had made the white man's bullets useless.

b. The Great Spirit would protect them from death.

c. Their guns were more powerful than the white man's guns.

d. The Great Spirit would reward them for their courage.

C. True or False. Write the word "true" or "false" next to each statement.

_____ 13. A territory could join the United States when it had the same number of settlers as a state.

_____ 14. Lewis and Clark found that the bears out west were smaller and not as aggressive as the bears they were used to seeing.

_____ 15. Not all Native Americans were hostile to the white settlers who began moving west.

_____ 16. The Shawnee and Choctaw tribes were successful in creating a confederacy against the white settlers.

D. Answer the following question using complete sentences.

17. What did the Prophet preach to the Native Americans?

_____

_____

_____

_____

_____

Name _____   Date _____

The Story of the World, Volume 3: Early Modern Times

Chapter 33 Test: The End of Napoleon

A. Fill in the blanks.

1. During the War of 1812, the British burned parts of _____.

2. The French asked Louis XVIII, the _____ of the guillotined king, to return France and rule in Napoleon's place.

3. When Napoleon finally admitted defeat, he was sent to the small island of _____ in the Mediterranean Sea.

4. Napoleon was defeated by the British in his last battle, the Battle of _____.

5. The British sent Napoleon to the island of _____, far off in the Atlantic Ocean.

B. Multiple Choice. Write the letter of the best choice.

____ 6. What two countries did the British convince to join with them in defying Napoleon?
  a. Austria and Denmark
  b. Spain and Portugal
  c. Russia and Sweden
  d. Austria and Russia

____ 7. Alexander I gave Napoleon part of _____ in exchange for peace.
  a. Prussia
  b. Russia
  c. Poland
  d. Italy

____ 8. How did Napoleon decide to defeat the British?
  a. He sent his navy across the English Channel.
  b. He closed off all European ports to the British.
  c. He bribed all of Britain's allies.
  d. He blockaded all of the British ports.

_____ 9. Why did the United States declare war on the British in 1812?

    a. The British had been raiding American ships for soldiers to fight Napoleon.

    b. The Americans wanted to capture more land in Canada.

    c. The British refused to sell goods to American merchants.

    d. all of the above

_____ 10. What happened to Tecumseh during the War of 1812?

    a. He fled to England.

    b. He succeeded in winning back some of the Shawnee land.

    c. He was killed in a battle with William Henry Harrison.

    d. The British gave him land for his tribe in Canada.

_____ 11. Why did the French people welcome Napoleon when he escaped his island and marched back to Paris?

    a. They missed having an emperor.

    b. They were afraid Louis XVIII would become another tyrant.

    c. They were frightened by Napoleon's massive army.

    d. They believed Napoleon had been sent by God to free them.

_____ 12. Who was the British commander who finally defeated Napoleon?

    a. Lord Byron

    b. The Duke of Windsor

    c. Admiral Nelson

    d. The Duke of Wellington

C. True or False. Write the word "true" or "false" next to each statement.

_____ 13. Napoleon ruled most of Europe, but he never managed to conquer Portugal.

_____ 14. During the War of 1812, Great Britain lost more land to the United States.

_____ 15. After his defeat, Napoleon wanted to go to America and study botany.

_____ 16. Tourists used to visit the island where Napoleon lived in exile.

_____ 17. Napoleon believed he had been poisoned by English assassins.

D. Answer the following questions using complete sentences.

18. What problems did Napoleon's army face as they left Moscow and marched back to France? How many of his men died on the march?

_____

_____

_____

_____

_____

The Story of the World, Volume 3: Early Modern Times

Chapter 34 Test: Freedom for South America

A. Fill in the blanks.

1. A _____ was a person born in the Spanish colonies.

2. _____ was the capital city of Venezuela.

3. The people of Venezuela gave Simón Bolívar the title _____.

4. José de San Martín drove the Spanish out of _____, the capital of Peru.

5. San Martín marched his army across the _____ Mountains.

6. The South American country of _____ was named in honor of Simón Bolívar.

B. Multiple Choice. Write the letter of the best choice.

_____ 7. Who first tried to convince the people of Venezuela to drive out the Spanish?
   a. Simón Bolívar
   b. Francisco de Miranda
   c. José de San Martín
   d. Joseph Bonaparte

_____ 8. How did Napoleon provide Venezuela with a chance to be free?
   a. He took the throne away from the Spanish king and occupied the Spanish army.
   b. He sent his brother with an army to help the people of Venezuela.
   c. He invaded Venezuela's neighbors.
   d. all of the above

_____ 9. Which South American colonies had already declared their independence?
   a. Paraguay and Uruguay
   b. Chile and New Granada
   c. Uruguay and Patagonia
   d. Paraguay and Argentina

_____ 10. Where did Bolívar go when he was forced to flee Venezuela the first time?

    a. New Granada

    b. Paraguay

    c. Argentina

    d. Chile

_____ 11. The Spanish convinced the _____ to fight against Bolívar.

    a. Africans

    b. poorer cowboys

    c. Native Americans

    d. wealthy landowners

_____ 12. Who helped Bolívar take back control of Venezuela from Spain the second time?

    a. the emperor of Haiti

    b. the English

    c. the new French king

    d. the United States

_____ 13. Which of the following was NOT one of the states in La Republica de Colombia?

    a. New Granada

    b. Venezuela

    c. Quito (Ecuador)

    d. Peru

_____ 14. What did San Martín want to do to convince his people he was a good leader?

    a. drive the Spanish out of all of the South American colonies

    b. capture Bolívar and turn him over to the Spanish

    c. unite the countries of South America

    d. take back a port that Bolívar had captured

C. True or False. Write the word "true" or "false" next to each statement.

_____ 15. Simón Bolívar was born in Spain but moved to Venezuela when he was six.

_____ 16. After Spain regained control of Venezuela, Bolívar fled to America.

_____ 17. The "Letter from Jamaica" detailed Bolívar's plans for the South American colonies to become states of one strong country.

_____ 18. Many rebel leaders in South America thought that Bolívar was too anxious for power.

_____ 19. Before Simón Bolívar died, he said that South Americans were not ready to be free.

D. Answer the following question using complete sentences.

20. Why was South America never able to unite?

_____

_____

_____

_____

_____

The Story of the World, Volume 3: Early Modern Times

Chapter 35 Test: Mexican Independence

A. Fill in the blanks.

1. In his speech called _____, Don Miguel told the people their lives were hard because of the Spanish and encouraged them to gain their freedom.

2. On September 16th, Mexico celebrates _____.

3. The group of army officers, led by Morelos, who claimed to be the rulers of New Spain were called a _____.

4. The Mexicans eventually decided that they would be ruled as a _____.

B. Multiple Choice. Write the letter of the best choice.

_____   5. Don Miguel was the _____ of Dolores.

   a. mayor

   b. doctor

   c. priest

   d. butcher

_____   6. Fray Estrada accused Don Miguel of _____.

   a. teaching strange, untrue beliefs instead of true Catholic doctrine

   b. spending his days drinking and amusing himself

   c. neglecting his church

   d. all of the above

_____   7. How did Don Miguel help the Indians of Dolores?

   a. He taught the Indians to make wine from his vineyard.

   b. He built a factory where the Indians could make pots and bricks to sell.

   c. He raised mulberry trees so that the Indians could make silk.

   d. all of the above

_____   8. Why did Don Miguel order his men to retreat when they reached Mexico City?

   a. He was afraid that the Spanish had set a trap for them.

   b. The Spanish leaders had bribed him to retreat.

   c. He was afraid they would kill innocent people as they did in Guanajuato.

   d. He knew the Spanish soldiers were too strong for them to defeat.

_____ 9. Who led the second revolt against Spain?

    a. Miguel Hidalgo

    b. José María Morelos y Pavón

    c. Agustín de Iturbide

    d. Antonio López de Santa Anna

_____ 10. Iturbide became Mexico's first _____.

    a. president

    b. emperor

    c. general

    d. pope

_____ 11. Who led the revolt against Iturbide?

    a. Miguel Hidalgo

    b. José María Morelos y Pavón

    c. Vincente Guerrero

    d. Antonio López de Santa Anna

_____ 12. What happened to Iturbide?

    a. Rebel soldiers killed him.

    b. He fled to Italy and died there.

    c. His enemies tricked him into returning to Mexico and then put him to death.

    d. He became the Mexican ambassador to the United States.

C. True or False. Write the word "true" or "false" next to each statement.

_____ 13. The French philosopher Voltaire wrote about the equality of all men and their right to rule themselves.

_____ 14. The peninsulares were the most powerful people in New Spain.

_____ 15. The Spanish army wanted to execute Don Miguel but never did because he was a priest.

_____ 16. Iturbide decided to fight with the rebels when Spain refused to honor him with a special medal.

_____ 17. Iturbide abused his power and threw the leaders of the Mexican congress in jail.

D. Answer the following question using complete sentences.

18. What were the Three Guarantees?

_____

_____

_____

_____

_____

The Story of the World, Volume 3: Early Modern Times

Chapter 36 Test: The Slave Trade Ends

A. Fill in the blanks.

1. _____ were men and women who wanted to make slavery illegal.

2. In England, a religious group called the _____ had insisted that slavery should be illegal for a long time.

3. Southerners in the United States needed slaves to work in their _____ and _____ fields.

4. _____ asked the British Parliament to outlaw the slave trade, no matter what the cost.

B. Multiple Choice. Write the letter of the best choice.

_____ 5. Why did the British Parliament refuse to make slavery illegal?

    a. Landowners said that they could not survive without slaves.

    b. No one believed the stories about how horrible slavery was.

    c. English merchant ships made too much money selling slaves.

    d. all of the above

_____ 6. What had to happen before slavery would become illegal?

    a. The slave trade had to be outlawed.

    b. Southerners had to find a new crop.

    c. Northerners had to find new workers for their factories.

    d. all of the above

_____ 7. What happened to many British planters when slavery was outlawed?

    a. They hired factory workers to work on their farms instead.

    b. They moved to India to start plantations there.

    c. They went bankrupt.

    d. They moved to the cities and began working in the factories.

_____ 8. After slavery was outlawed, the British began to buy goods such as sugar, cotton, and tobacco from _____.

    a. India

    b. China

    c. the United States.

    d. South America

C. True or False. Write the word "true" or "false" next to each statement.

_____ 9. Former slaves published stories of their lives to tell people about the plight of the slaves.

_____ 10. The United States was the first country to pass a law that made it illegal to buy slaves in Africa and then sell them in other countries.

_____ 11. More people owned slaves in the Southern part of the United States than in the North.

D. Answer the following question using complete sentences.

12. What did the Constitution of the United States say about slaves?

_____

_____

_____

_____

_____

Name _____   Date _____

Chapter 37 Test: Troubled Africa

A. Fill in the blanks.

1. Africa was known to many Europeans as _____.

2. Shaka was king of the _____ tribe.

3. The period of ten years during which Shaka spread his rule throughout Africa is called _____ by Africans.

4. The Dutch had a settlement in South Africa called _____.

5. The Dutch who lived there called themselves _____, which means "farmers" in Dutch.

B. Multiple Choice. Write the letter of the best choice.

_____ 6. Why do we know less about African history than about English history?

    a. The English were not able to translate African texts.

    b. African tribes did not use writing to record their history.

    c. African historical documents were destroyed during numerous wars.

    d. People have lived in England longer than they have in Africa.

_____ 7. When two English traders wanted to build a trading post in southern Africa, they needed permission from _____.

    a. the king of England

    b. Shaka

    c. the Dutch

    d. the East India Company

_____ 8. The traders named their new trading post _____.

    a. Natal

    b. Mtetwa

    c. Durban

    d. Bombay

_____ 9. After Shaka became king of his tribe and improved the army, who was his first target?

    a. his mother's family

    b. his father's family

    c. the Dutch settlers

    d. the English traders

_____ 10. Shaka was murdered by _____.

    a. two of his sons

    b. his half-brothers

    c. his army commander

    d. his warriors

_____ 11. When the British conquered the Dutch settlement in South Africa, what did they do that greatly angered many of the Dutch people living there?

    a. They made slavery illegal.

    b. They forced the Dutch to pay taxes to the British king.

    c. They made English the official language of the colony.

    d. They persecuted the Dutch Catholics.

_____ 12. When the Dutch settlers moved and attempted to make friends with the native Africans, what did the new African king do?

    a. He welcomed them and gave a great feast in their honor.

    b. He made them sign a treaty promising not to take any more land.

    c. He told them to go home.

    d. He ordered them all put to death.

C. True or False. Write the word "true" or "false" next to each statement.

_____ 13. Shaka brought peace to many people in South Africa.

_____ 14. When Shaka was a boy, he was not welcome with either his father's family or his mother's family.

_____ 15. When Shaka's mother died, he went mad.

_____ 16. When the Dutch left their first settlement and journeyed into the unknown depths of Africa, it was known as the Trail of Tears.

_____ 17. The Dutch established two nations in South Africa called the Orange Free State and the Transvaal Republic.

D. Answer the following question using complete sentences.

18. What changes did Shaka make in his army to make it stronger?

_____

_____

_____

_____

_____

The Story of the World, Volume 3: Early Modern Times

Chapter 38 Test: American Tragedies

A. Fill in the blanks.

1. President _____ signed the Indian Removal Act.

2. The Chickasaw, Choctaw, Seminole, Cherokee, and the Creek Indians were known as the Five _____ because so many of them lived just like white settlers.

3. The Cherokee's forced journey to Oklahoma is known as the _____.

4. When Nat Turner saw a _____, he felt it was a sign that it was time for the slaves to break free.

B. Multiple Choice. Write the letter of the best choice.

____ 5. When American settlers wanted to build houses on Native American land, what were they supposed to do?
   a. Make sure no Native Americans were living there first.
   b. Ask the Native American chief for permission.
   c. Ask the United States government for permission.
   d. Pay for the land and sign a treaty explaining that the Native Americans had agreed to sell it.

____ 6. The Indian Removal Act said that the President could now take Native American land without asking for it, as long as he _____.
   a. gave the Native Americans an equal amount of land in the unsettled west
   b. paid the Native Americans a fair price
   c. got approval from Congress first
   d. all of the above

____ 7. The _____ tribe went to war and fought the U.S. for seven years.
   a. Choctaw
   b. Seminole
   c. Cherokee
   d. Creek

_____ 8. The _____ went to court to try to keep their homes.
   a. Choctaw
   b. Seminole
   c. Cherokee
   d. Creek

_____ 9. When planters in the south heard stories about _____, they became very worried.
   a. the French Revolution
   b. the bankrupt planters in England
   c. South American rebels
   d. the revolt on St. Dominigue

_____ 10. The _____ told the slaves about a coming time of freedom when God would heal all the suffering of the slaves.
   a. abolitionists
   b. white ministers
   c. black ministers
   d. Quaker missionaries

_____ 11. What did Nat Turner and his men decide to do when they met whites?
   a. kill them all
   b. kill only the men
   c. burn their houses
   d. take them prisoner

_____ 12. What finally happened to Nat Turner and his men?
   a. They were captured and returned to their masters.
   b. They escaped on the Underground Railroad.
   c. They were captured and executed.
   d. They fled to Haiti.

C. True or False. Write the word "true" or "false" next to each statement.

_____ 13. The Chickasaw and Choctaw Indians fought the hardest to keep their homes.

_____ 14. Slaves in the American south had even less freedom than the Indians.

_____ 15. Nat Turner led his revolt in the state of South Carolina.

_____ 16. Nat Turner's story was published by his lawyer, Thomas Gray.

D. Answer the following question using complete sentences.

17. What happened to slaves as a result of Turner's rebellion?

_____

_____

_____

_____

_____

The Story of the World, Volume 3: Early Modern Times

Chapter 39 Test: China Adrift

A. Multiple Choice. Write the letter of the best choice.

_____ 1. During the end of Chi'en-lung's reign, he gave power to Ho-Shen, his _____.

    a. son

    b. favorite army officer

    c. grandson

    d. wife

_____ 2. Why were people concerned that Ho-Shen was gaining power?

    a. He was a corrupt liar.

    b. He wanted to put a stop to the opium trade.

    c. The officials knew they could not bribe him to get what they wanted.

    d. all of the above

_____ 3. Why did Chi'en-lung give his throne to Pinyin Jiqing?

    a. He wanted Pinyin Jiqing to get some experience before he died.

    b. He was worried that Ho-Shen might try to steal the throne when he died.

    c. He was tired and wanted to retire to a monastery.

    d. He thought it would be disrespectful to rule longer than the greatest Manchu ruler.

_____ 4. What was Pinyin Jiqing's new, royal name?

    a. Lin Zexu

    b. Tao-Kung

    c. Chia-ch'ing

    d. K'ang-hsi

_____ 5. What did Pinyin Jiqing do to Ho-Shen?

    a. He banished Ho-Shen from China.

    b. He allowed Ho-Shen to commit honorable suicide.

    c. He killed Ho-Shen.

    d. He made Ho-Shen the commander of his army.

_____ 6. People from _____ were smuggling opium into China.

    a. the United States

    b. Britain

    c. France

    d. Japan

_____ 7. One official suggested that opium be made legal so that _____.

    a. The money from opium would stay in China.

    b. The pirates who smuggled opium would leave.

    c. The Chinese people would not want so much of it.

    d. all of the above

_____ 8. How did Lin Zexu attempt to wipe out the opium problem?

    a. He sent out orders for sixty Chinese opium merchants to be thrown in jail.

    b. He threatened to close all Chinese ports forever unless every ship in Canton handed over all their opium.

    c. He threatened to arrest and put to death any British merchant found trading opium.

    d. all of the above

_____ 9. What did Lin Zexu do with the opium that he recovered?

    a. He burned it and then buried the ashes.

    b. He dumped it into three large holes, flooded the holes, and washed it all away.

    c. He sent it to Hong Kong.

    d. He sold it to the Japanese.

B. True or False. Write the word "true" or "false" next to each statement.

_____ 10. The Chinese spent so much money on opium that they started to run short of silver coins.

_____ 11. Lin Zexu's nickname was "Blue Sky" because he was as pure as a cloudless sky.

_____ 12. The Chinese had a strong navy with many warships.

_____ 13. The Chinese called the Treaty of Nanjing the "unequal treaty."

C. Answer the following question using complete sentences.

14. What did the Treaty of Nanjing require of the Chinese?

_____

_____

_____

_____

_____

_____

The Story of the World, Volume 3: Early Modern Times

Chapter 40 Test: Mexico and Her Neighbor

A. Fill in the blanks.

1. The Americans who lived in Texas were called _____.

2. _____ was the quick-tempered frontiersman who became the general of the new Texas army.

3. _____ was the commander of the American soldiers at the Alamo.

4. _____ was a young congressman from Illinois who opposed the war with Mexico.

5. The young captain who led the U.S. to victory near Mexico City was _____.

B. Multiple Choice. Write the letter of the best choice.

____ 6. American settlements in Spanish land were known as _____.

     a. garrisons

     b. empresarios

     c. missions

     d. encomiendas

____ 7. When an American settled in Mexico, he was supposed to _____.

     a. become a Mexican citizen

     b. convert to Catholicism

     c. obey Mexican laws

     d. all of the above

____ 8. When Santa Anna became dictator, he passed a law that said _____.

     a. no one in Texas could own slaves

     b. no one in Texas could have a gun unless the Mexican government gave him permission

     c. no more Americans could move to Texas

     d. Spanish would be the official language of Texas

_____ 9. What did the commander of the San Antonio fighters do when Santa Anna's men surrounded the Alamo?

    a. He raised a white flag to surrender.

    b. He sent a soldier out to try to negotiate with Santa Anna.

    c. He stood firm and decided to fight.

    d. He raised a red flag which meant, "Surrender without conditions!"

_____ 10. President Jackson proposed that Mexico _____.

    a. send Santa Anna to Washington to discuss a peace treaty

    b. sell Texas to the United States

    c. give up Texas peacefully before more men were killed

    d. allow the citizens of Texas to vote on which country they would belong to

_____ 11. The U.S. declared war on Mexico to claim Texas and _____.

    a. to capture Santa Anna and execute him

    b. to get revenge for the Alamo

    c. to make Texas a free country

    d. to drive the Mexicans from North America

C. True or False. Write the word "true" or "false" next to each statement.

_____ 12. During the battle of the Alamo, all of the 189 Texans were killed, but 600 Mexican soldiers were killed as well.

_____ 13. Most Texans were eager to become part of the United States.

_____ 14. Slavery was illegal in the new state of Texas.

_____ 15. The treaty with Mexico gave the U.S. the piece of land where California, Nevada, Utah, Arizona, Colorado, New Mexico, and Wyoming now lie.

D. Answer the following question using complete sentences.

16. Why did the Mexicans become annoyed with the Americans who lived in Texas?

_____

_____

_____

_____

_____

The Story of the World, Volume 3: Early Modern Times

Chapter 41 Test: New Zealand and Her Rulers

A. Fill in the blanks.

1. The native people of New Zealand called themselves the Maori which meant _____.

2. They called the English pakehas which meant _____.

3. In 1844, a ship brought two flocks of _____ to New Zealand.

4. _____ was a Maori chief who rebelled against the British.

B. Multiple Choice. Write the letter of the best choice.

_____ 5. What did the Maori receive in trade from the British settlers?

    a. wild game

    b. guns

    c. spears and axes

    d. sweet potatoes

_____ 6. What disease did the Maori catch from the settlers?

    a. smallpox

    b. measles

    c. influenza

    d. all of the above

_____ 7. What did the missionaries and settlers beg the British to do?

    a. stop the Australians from coming to New Zealand

    b. defend them against attacks by the Maori

    c. seize land from the Maori so that they could have it

    d. come and turn New Zealand into a law-abiding place

_____ 8. The British promised to protect the rights and property of the Maori if the Maori would _____.

    a. sell most of their land to the settlers

    b. stop attacking the English settlers

    c. recognize England as their ruler

    d. all of the above

_____ 9. What did the British governor tell the Maori when some of them tried to sell land?

    a. They were not allowed to sell their land.

    b. The British already owned the land.

    c. They could only sell land to the British government.

    d. They had to get the price approved by the British governor.

_____ 10. What did the Maori do to the British at Kororareka four different times?

    a. They killed the British governor.

    b. They burned the settlement.

    c. They cut down the flagpole.

    d. They stole the settlers' animals.

C. True or False. Write the word "true" or "false" next to each statement.

_____ 11. If a country has annexed land, it has purchased that land for itself.

_____ 12. The British promised that if the Maori would give New Zealand to the British, the British could make laws that would protect them from white invasion.

_____ 13. After the British came to New Zealand, most of the Maori moved to the South Island.

_____ 14. The Maori burned the British settlement at Kororareka.

_____ 15. For thirty years, the Maori and the British fought a series of wars over the land of New Zealand.

D. Answer the following question using complete sentences.

16. How were the two versions of the Treaty of Waitangi different?

_____

_____

_____

_____

_____

Name _____   Date _____

The Story of the World, Volume 3: Early Modern Times

Chapter 42 Test: The World of Forty-Nine

A. Fill in the blanks.

1. The Spanish found gold in _____, and the Americans found gold in _____.

2. The _____ fought against the English in Australia, and the _____ fought against the English in New Zealand.

3. The cities of 1850 had beautiful buildings at their centers and _____ around their edges.

4. In 1850, the slaveowners in the U.S. quarreled with the _____ who wanted to make slavery illegal.

B. Multiple Choice. Write the letter of the best choice.

_____ 5. John Sutter hired Jim Marshall to _____.

    a. pan for gold

    b. open a trading post

    c. build a sawmill

    d. oversee his farm

_____ 6. Marshall and his men found gold in the American River in the _____.

    a. Klondike

    b. Sacramento Valley

    c. Death Valley

    d. Shenandoah Valley

_____ 7. How did Marshall test the gold to see if it was real?

    a. He bit it with his teeth.

    b. He burned it.

    c. He hammered it out.

    d. He took it to a bank.

141

_____ 8. What did Sam Brannan sell when he discovered there was gold at Sutter's Mill?

    a. land

    b. blue jeans

    c. dynamite

    d. picks and pans

_____ 9. When a person in California wanted to claim land as his own, what did he do?

    a. put a fence around it

    b. asked the government for permission

    c. drove a stake in the ground

    d. all of the above

_____ 10. People came to California from _____.

    a. England and France

    b. China

    c. Germany and Sweden

    d. all of the above

C. True or False. Write the word "true" or "false" next to each statement.

_____ 11. Most of the miners who traveled to California became rich.

_____ 12. After gold was discovered, the population of California grew from fifteen thousand people to over a hundred thousand in less than two years.

_____ 13. When California joined the United States in 1850, it was the richest state in the Union.

_____ 14. In 1850, there were only a few railroads in the United States and Europe.

D. Answer the following question using complete sentences.

15. In 1850, why was the world full of unrest?

_____

_____

_____

_____

_____

_____

_____

Answer Key

Chapter 1 Test

1. Philip
2. Ferdinand I
3. Charlemagne
4. conquistadores
5. encomiendas
6. b
7. d
8. c
9. a
10. d
11. b
12. a
13. false
14. true
15. false
16. true
17. false
18. The Spanish took jewelry away from the native tribes. They panned for gold in the streams, and they dug mines into the ground.

Chapter 2 Test

1. Philip II
2. William the Silent
3. dikes
4. Holland
5. d
6. b
7. c
8. b
9. a
10. b
11. d
12. d
13. false
14. false
15. true
16. true
17. true
18. The Netherlands seemed far away to the people who lived in the large cities of Spain and Italy, so they called it the Netherlands, which means "far-away lands." The Netherlands were also known as the Low Countries because they were below the level of the ocean.

Chapter 3 Test

1. James I, England; James VI, Scotland
2. Puritans
3. Discovery, Godspeed, Susan Constant
4. a
5. c
6. c
7. b
8. c
9. c
10. a
11. d
12. d
13. false
14. false
15. true
16. true
17. John Smith was frustrated with the Jamestown colonists because they spent all of their time searching for gold. He thought they needed to do other work before their food supplies ran out, and he wanted them to build walls around their settlement to protect themselves.

Chapter 4 Test

1. Canada
2. Quebec
3. Hudson Bay OR Hudson Strait
4. d
5. c
6. d
7. b
8. a
9. a
10. d
11. true
12. false
13. true
14. false
15. The Northwest Passage was a river that would run all the way through North America, from the Atlantic Ocean on one side to the Pacific Ocean on the other. Explorers wanted to find it so they could get to China and India and grow wealthy trading for silks and spices.

Chapter 5 Test

1. c
2. d
3. a
4. b
5. c
6. b
7. a
8. b
9. d
10. c
11. c
12. c
13. a
14. d
15. false
16. false
17. true
18. false
19. Ieyasu forced every daimyo to destroy all of the castles in his territory except for the one where the daimyo actually lived. That way the daimyo could not build up a secret army in a hidden fortress. Ieyasu also forced the daimyo to swear oaths of loyalty to him, and he forced them to move their families to the capital city. Ieyasu gave the samurai new jobs so that they would not fight against him.

Chapter 6 Test

1. Mayflower
2. Squanto
3. Plymouth Plantation
4. Peter Stuyvesant
5. New York
6. d
7. b
8. c
9. b
10. d
11. b
12. b
13. false
14. true
15. false
16. true
17. true
18. The Mayflower Compact was a set of laws that the Pilgrims drew up for their new colony. It said that all colonists must agree together before a law could be passed, and that once laws were passed, each colonist would obey them.

Chapter 7 Test

1. John Rolfe
2. indentured servants
3. Dutch
4. Angola
5. b
6. d
7. b
8. a
9. d
10. a
11. d
12. b
13. false
14. false
15. true
16. false
17. true
18. Tobacco farming was hard work because the seeds had to be hand-planted, hand-weeded, and hand-pruned. Worms had to be picked off one at a time. At harvest time, the leaves had to be taken off one at a time and hung on pegs to dry. Then the stems had to be taken off and the leaves had to be packed into barrels.

Chapter 8 Test

1. Babylon
2. Persia
3. Alexander the Great
4. Parthia
5. Islamic Empire
6. Mongols
9. a
10. a
11. b
12. a
13. b
14. true
15. false
16. false
17. false
18. When Murad inherited the throne of the Ottomans, his empire had grown too large. The previous sultans had spent too much money on feasts, palaces, and silks. Spanish gold had become more valuable than the Ottoman silver, and the Ottoman officials were corrupt. The Ottomans had even lost control of Baghdad.

Chapter 9 Test

1. b
2. d
3. b
4. c
5. d
6. a
7. c
8. a
9. d
10. d
11. b
12. a
13. a
14. d
15. true
16. false
17. true
18. true
19. true
20. King Gustavus trained his soldiers to fight in small groups instead of in a long line. He paid them well so that they would remain loyal to him. He gave them the best and warmest clothes, and he put them all in the same uniform so they could easily recognize each other in battle.

Chapter 10 Test

1. Buddhist
2. Jesuits
3. Zen Buddhists
4. Peking
5. b
6. d
7. c
8. c
9. b
10. b
11. a
12. false
13. true
14. true
15. true
16. true
17. The Ming Empire was attacked by the Manchu people to the north. China also was growing very poor due to the large amount of money the Chinese had spent fighting the Japanese. There were too many people in China and not enough farm land to grow food for them.

Chapter 11 Test

1. b
2. c
3. a
4. b
5. a
6. c
7. d
8. b
9. c
10. b
11. a
12. d
13. d
14. true
15. false
16. true
17. true
18. false
19. false
20. Aurangzeb refused to give Hindus positions at court and forced them to pay extra taxes. He destroyed Hindu temple and he made wine and festivals illegal.

Chapter 12 Test

1. Cavaliers
2. Roundheads
3. monarchy
4. commonwealth
5. Lord Protector
6. d
7. b
8. d
9. c
10. c
11. c
12. c
13. true
14. true
15. false
16. false
17. false
18. false
19. The people did not like Oliver Cromwell because he ordered his soldiers to destroy the royal regalia used to crown kings, and he allowed them to wreck churches that seemed too "Catholic." He outlawed cardplaying and closed all of the theatres in England.

Chapter 13 Test

1. Louis XIII
2. France
3. Versailles
4. sun
5. a
6. c
7. b
8. b
9. a
10. d
11. c
12. true
13. false
14. true
15. true
16. true
17. Versailles was a quarter of a mile long and had a Grand Canal that ran through the grounds. Inside the palace were elaborate rooms such as the Hall of Mirrors where seventeen huge mirrors stood across from seventeen large windows, and the Salon of Apollo, where a solid silver throne stood. The garden was full of statues of Greek gods with Louis XIV's face.

Chapter 14 Test

1. Brandenburg
2. Reich
3. Frederick William I
4. Frederick the Great
5. d
6. b
7. c
8. b
9. c
10. c
11. a
12. b
13. false
14. false
15. true
16. Frederick acted like a great king and gave elaborate feasts and parties. He also founded a Prussian university and the Prussian Academy of the Arts and the Royal Prussian Academy of Sciences. He had the academy teach the people how to speak the German language properly.

Chapter 15 Test

1. King Philip's War
2. Marie-Madeleine
3. Quakers
4. Pennsylvania; Philadelphia
5. b
6. c
7. a
8. d
9. c
10. d
11. a
12. b
13. true
14. true
15. false
16. false
17. true
18. The Quakers were a religious group that refused to belong to the Church of England. Instead they gathered together in plain meetinghouses where they sat and prayed quietly, waiting for God's words to come directly into their hearts. They believed that every man and woman should be equal, and they believed that fighting was wrong.

Chapter 16 Test

1. scientific method
2. gravity
3. Enlightenment
4. Agricultural
5. c
6. a
7. b
8. b
9. d
10. b
11. a
12. b
13. false
14. true
15. true
16. false
17. John Locke said that a good government should have three parts. One part would make the laws, another part would enforce those laws, and the third part would be in charge of fighting wars with other countries.

Chapter 17 Test

1. czar
2. Baltic
3. St. Petersburg
4. Europe
5. b
6. c
7. a
8. b
9. a
10. c
11. d
12. d
13. true
14. true
15. false
16. false
17. true
18. Peter the Great built canals, factories, salt works, iron mills, and mines. He brought European craftsmen to Russia to teach Russians how to make cloth, lacquer ware, and other goods. He made St. Petersburg into a great city filled with magnificent palaces.

Chapter 18 Test

1. sultan
2. Janissaries
3. Vienna
4. vizier
5. Tulip King
6. a
7. b
8. d
9. a
10. d
11. b
12. c
13. false
14. true
15. false
16. false
17. true
18. Ahmet III built a new palace that was modeled after a French palace. His prime minister sent ambassadors to French cities to find out more about Western art and science. They brought back a printing press so that the Turks could publish their own books.

Chapter 19 Test

1. Delhi
2. Ali
3. East India Company
4. Bombay
5. Sir Robert Clive
6. b
7. c
8. c
9. b
10. b
11. d
12. a
13. false
14. true
15. true
16. true
17. The English army that took over India was sent by the East India Company. This was unusual because the East India Company wasn't a country or a king. It was a company whose members hired an army and a general to lead it.

Chapter 20 Test

1. Peking
2. Manchu
3. Yellow; Yangtze
4. dragon
5. Gobi Desert
6. b
7. d
8. d
9. b
10. b
11. a
12. c
13. false
14. true
15. true
16. false
17. false
18. true
19. Copying the books in Chi'en-lung's series was difficult because there were over 36,000 volumes in the set and each volume had to be copied by hand. Another challenge was that the Chinese language had so many symbols for different sounds and letters—over 40,000 symbols.

Chapter 21 Test

1. d
2. a
3. c
4. b
5. c
6. b
7. a
8. d
9. a
10. d
11. c
12. d
13. b
14. d
15. b
16. true
17. false
18. false
19. true
20. At the beginning of the French and Indian War, the French were used to fighting in the woods and the English were not. The English soldiers' red coats made them easy targets for the French, and the English general insisted that his men march and fight in a straight line. Later the English turned their red coats inside out and covered the insides with clay. They rubbed soot and dirt on their shiny guns so that they wouldn't glint in the sun, and they started fighting in small groups, from behind trees.

Chapter 22 Test

1. George III
2. Patrick Henry
3. Boston Massacre
4. George Washington
5. Bunker Hill
6. Thomas Jefferson
7. c
8. b
9. d
10. c
11. a
12. a
13. a
14. true
15. false
16. false
17. true
18. false
19. true
20. According to British law, no British citizen could be forced to pay a tax unless his representative in Parliament agreed. But since there were no Americans in Parliament, the colonies didn't have representatives. So the colonists argued that Parliament should not pass laws that forced them to pay taxes.

Chapter 23 Test

1. constitution
2. federal
3. Congress, Senate, House of Representatives
4. Cabinet
5. b
6. d
7. b
8. b
9. c
10. c
11. a
12. c
13. false
14. true
15. false
16. true
17. true
18. false
19. The Bill of Rights is a list of powers that the government can never use against the people of the United States—such as forbidding American citizens to speak their opinions, to worship God as they please, to assemble together in public, or to keep weapons to defend themselves. The Bill of Rights said the federal government could never behave like a king toward its people—even if there seemed to be good reasons for doing so.

Chapter 24 Test

1. Venus
2. Botany Bay
3. New South Wales
4. hulks
5. Sydney
6. Aborigines
7. b
8. d
9. b
10. c
11. a
12. d
13. b
14. false
15. true
16. false
17. false
18. true
19. Life was difficult for the squatters in Australia. They had to fight off burning sun, drought, unexpected floods, and loneliness. There were no doctors, no stores, and no towns, and the squatters only got mail two times each year when the supply wagons came.

Chapter 25 Test

1. Marie Antoinette
2. National Assembly
3. Tennis Court Oath
4. Bastille
5. Citizen
6. c
7. b
8. d
9. d
10. a
11. b
12. c
13. false
14. true
15. true
16. true
17. false
18. Roman Catholic priests belonged to the First Estate. The noblemen of France belonged to the Second Estate. All of the merchants, shopkeepers, doctors, farmers, lawyers, judges, peasants, bakers, tailors, and cobblers of France belonged to the Third Estate.

Chapter 26 Test

1. Germany, Sweden
2. smallpox
3. Prussian
4. Metropolitan
5. b
6. d
7. d
8. d
9. a
10. c
11. d
12. false
13. true
14. true
15. true
16. false
17. Catherine the Great rewrote Russia's laws so that her people would have more rights. She told her ministers of state that no one could be tortured for information. She opened new schools and started the first college for Russian women. She also opened new hospitals and brought in doctors from the West to improve the health of the Russian people.

Chapter 27 Test

1. James Watt
2. coal
3. southern
4. cotton gin
5. standardization
6. d
7. a
8. c
9. d
10. a
11. b
12. d
13. false
14. true
15. true
16. false
17. true
18. The steam engine changed many things in England, Europe, and North America. Steam could run so many more machines so much more quickly than human muscles, windmills, or waterwheels. Ships and trains could haul heavy loads and carry more passengers. More and more coal had to be mined to power the steam engines, and railroads were built across farmland to haul more coal.

Chapter 28 Test

1. Confucius
2. Canton OR Guangzhou
3. George Macartney
4. kowtow
5. poppy
6. d
7. a
8. c
9. d
10. b
11. c
12. a
13. false
14. true
15. true
16. true
17. false
18. The Eight Regulations were laws that foreigners who came to China had to follow. No foreign women were allowed to visit the warehouses on the dock at Canton. Foreign merchants had to ask Chinese merchants to speak to officials for them. Traders had to leave China at the end of the trading season and go home. Foreigners were forbidden to buy Chinese books or learn the Chinese language.

Chapter 29 Test

1. Ancients, Five Hundred
2. Director
3. Louisiana Territory
4. Admiral Horatio Nelson
5. Trafalgar
6. c
7. a
8. b
9. a
10. b
11. a
12. b
13. false
14. false
15. true
16. true
17. false
18. Napoleon wrote the new constitution. It said that Napoleon could make any laws he wanted, declare wars, and decide on France's policies all by himself.

Chapter 30 Test

1. sugar cane
2. coffee
3. Yellow fever OR Malaria
4. Haiti
5. c
6. b
7. d
8. b
9. c
10. c
11. d
12. true
13. false
14. true
15. true
16. French law said that a slave who earned his freedom had the rights of any Frenchman. Slaves in St. Domingue had no rights at all. The laws of St. Domingue said that everyone with African blood, slave or free, had to wear different clothes, sit in different parts of churches and other buildings, and be inside by nine o'clock every night. No one with African blood could become a goldsmith, jeweler, an army officer, or a doctor.

Chapter 31 Test

1. steam power
2. overseer
3. mills
4. General Ned Ludd
5. Boston, New York
6. b
7. c
8. d
9. d
10. a
11. c
12. true
13. true
14. false
15. false
16. In factories, workers did only one task over and over again. In the home, a worker did all of the jobs, from beginning to end.

Chapter 32 Test

1. Jefferson
2. Sacagawea
3. Continental Divide
4. Tecumseh
5. William Henry Harrison
6. c
7. d
8. b
9. a
10. d
11. c
12. a
13. true
14. false
15. true
16. false
17. The Prophet warned the Native Americans that they would lose their land forever if they continued to behave like the white men. He told them not to drink the white man's alcohol or wear their wool and cotton clothes. He told them not to sign treaties with the white men because no one owned the land, and he warned them not to marry white people.

Chapter 33 Test

1. Washington, D.C.
2. brother
3. Elba
4. Waterloo
5. St. Helena
6. d
7. c
8. b
9. a
10. c
11. b
12. d
13. true
14. false
15. true
16. true
17. true
18. When Napoleon's army left Moscow and marched back to France, it was winter and the temperature dropped, but the soldiers only had their summer uniforms. They could not find any food because they had burned the countryside on their march in. The Russians had burned all of the bridges between Russia and Poland. Six hundred thousand men died on the march home.

Chapter 34 Test

1. creole
2. Caracas
3. El Libertador OR The Liberator
4. Lima
5. Andes
6. Bolivia
7. b
8. a
9. d
10. a
11. b
12. a
13. d
14. d
15. false
16. false
17. true
18. true
19. false
20. South America was never able to unite because there was too much fighting going on inside each country. The creoles insisted on ruling over the Native Americans. The Native Americans fought with the descendents of African slaves. The "pure blooded" Spanish and Indians fought with those who were only part Indian or part African. The landowners and army officers were too busy quarrelling with each other to unite together under leaders who could make South America great.

Chapter 35 Test

1. The Cry of Dolores OR El Grito de Dolores
2. Independence Day
3. junta
4. republic
5. c
6. d
7. d
8. c
9. b
10. b
11. d
12. c
13. true
14. true
15. false
16. true
17. true
18. The Three Guarantees were Iturbide's ideas for New Spain. He said that New Spain should become a new, independent kingdom called Mexico, with its own king. All of its people would be equal, no matter where they were born or who they were. And Roman Catholicism would be the official religion of Mexico.

Chapter 36 Test

1. abolitionists
2. Quakers
3. cotton, tobacco
4. William Wilberforce
5. c
6. a
7. c
8. c
9. true
10. false
11. true
12. The Constitution said that slaves were not really people. When states counted their people, five slaves would count as three whole people.

Chapter 37 Test

1. the dark continent
2. Zulu
3. mfecane OR Time of Troubles
4. Cape Colony
5. Boers
6. b
7. b
8. c
9. a
10. b
11. a
12. d
13. false
14. true
15. true
16. false
17. true
18. Shaka changed the weapons that the soldiers used. He ordered them to fight with short stabbing spears instead of throwing spears, so that they would have to grapple with the enemy face to face. He sent them to walk on thorns with their bare feet, so that their soles would be tough enough to run over any rough land. He also gave them uniforms to wear, and he divided them into four sections and taught them to attack in the same order during each battle.

Chapter 38 Test

1. Andrew Jackson
2. Civilized Tribes
3. Trail of Tears
4. solar eclipse
5. d
6. a
7. b
8. c
9. d
10. c
11. a
12. c
13. false
14. true
15. false
16. true
17. As a result of Turner's rebellion, slaves were worse off than ever. Laws were passed keeping slaves from meeting together in groups of more than three. Black ministers were told that they couldn't preach to their congregations. Anyone who taught a slave to read or write would be punished by a year in jail. Free African-Americans were not allowed to own guns or to meet together at night unless three white men were present at all times.

Chapter 39 Test

1. b
2. a
3. d
4. c
5. b
6. b
7. a
8. d
9. b
10. true
11. true
12. false
13. true
14. The Treaty of Nanjing forced China to pay Great Britain twenty-one million dollars for the opium that had been destroyed. The Chinese also had to allow British ships to trade in five more ports. China had to allow English merchants to build settlements and live in China year round. The whole island of Hong Kong had to be given to the British. Finally, China had to agree to make the same treaty with France and the United States.

Chapter 40 Test

1. Anglos
2. Sam Houston
3. William Travis
4. Abraham Lincoln
5. Robert E. Lee
6. b
7. d
8. b
9. c
10. b
11. d
12. true
13. false
14. false
15. true
16. The Mexicans grew annoyed with the Americans living in Texas because there began to be more English-speaking Americans living in Texas than Spanish. Many of the Americans refused to be Catholic or follow Mexican laws. Worst of all, Americans insisted on bringing their slaves to Texas, even though slavery was illegal in Mexico.

Chapter 41 Test

1. ordinary people
2. white strangers
3. sheep
4. Hone Heke
5. b
6. d
7. d
8. c
9. c
10. c
11. false
12. true
13. false
14. false
15. true
16. The Maori version of the Treaty of Waitangi only gave the British the right to govern the lands—to rule them as long as the Maori agreed with their actions. The British version of the treaty said that the British had sovereignty, or complete control over the Maori lands.

Chapter 42 Test

1. South America, California
2. Aborigines, Maori
3. slums
4. abolitionists
5. c
6. b
7. c
8. d
9. c
10. d
11. false
12. true
13. true
14. false
15. In 1850, the English ruled over parts of Australia, New Zealand, India, and China—but the people in those countries wanted the English to leave. In South America, dictators and generals were trying to seize power. In the United States, slave owners argued with abolitionists. In Russia, hungry peasants resented the riches of the czar.